Effective Practice Group Leadership

Second Edition

EDITED BY ALEX DAVIES

Commissioning editor
Alex Davies

Managing director
Sian O'Neill

Effective Practice Group Leadership, Second Edition
is published by

Globe Law and Business Ltd
3 Mylor Close
Horsell
Woking
Surrey GU21 4DD
United Kingdom
Tel: +44 20 3745 4770
www.globelawandbusiness.com

Effective Practice Group Leadership, Second Edition

ISBN 9781787428690
EPUB ISBN 9781787428706
Adobe PDF ISBN 9781787428713

Contents

Executive summary

Law firm practice group leadership is not for the faint hearted. As firms compete increasingly at practice group level, leaders are being asked to run their groups like business units; to develop and implement a strategic plan that supports the goals and competitiveness of the firm; and to coordinate and lead their partners to enhance the efficiency, performance, and profitability of their groups. Many firm leaders complain that some of their group heads are not producing the results they want to see. But how many practice group leaders receive the tools and support they need to succeed in this critical role? How many are selected for demonstrable leadership skills? And how often are they held accountable for how well – or otherwise – they perform in the role?

With contributions from a wide range of experts, this second edition of *Effective Practice Group Leadership* explores these key questions and more, building on the first edition with new insights and thought leadership. The book examines the position of the practice group leader (PGL) in law firms today, the challenges of the role, and the changes to it, innovations and how modern practice groups are changing, and demonstrates the enormous contribution PGLs can make to the profitability and performance of their law firms, when armed with the tools and the authority.

Practice groups in law firms most often operate as important "business units" within a firm's broader departmental structure. It is often at the practice group level that firms do their budgeting and revenue tracking, hiring and training, business development, and marketing. This has made the role of practice group leader increasingly important, but also much more challenging to do well. Our opening chapter by Susan Saltonstall Duncan, president of RainMaking Oasis, sets the stage for the book, examining the practice group leader's general traits and skills, their role and responsibility as strategist and financial steward, as talent manager and coach, as well as steps to accelerate practice group leader effectiveness.

Next, Susan Raridon Lambreth, principal at LawVision Group, and Dr Larry Richard, founder and principal consultant at LawyerBrain LLC (and the leading expert on the psychology of lawyer behavior) explain why *every* practice group leader must be a change agent – *especially* if their group has a strong track record of comfortable, complacency-inducing growth. This chapter highlights several important characteristics of change agents, with advice on how you can implement or work on each one.

Law firms and practice groups are seeing dramatic changes in what clients want. They are also seeing increased competition from non-law firm service providers, including the accounting and consulting firms. Rather than fear the changes, practice group leaders must focus on major opportunities and, in the process, expand the roles of their practice groups into providing multi-disciplinary, turnkey services for clients. Chapter three by Michael Roster, former general counsel of Stanford University and former managing partner of Morrison & Foerster's Los Angeles office, discusses the opportunities and challenges for such business strategies, and possible ways to make the transition.

For years, innovation was genuinely discussed in law firm/client review meetings in the mutual (though) unexpressed understanding that neither side would be taken up on their proposals. It wasn't that innovation was feared or that both sides were necessarily wed to the status quo. It was just that everyone was *too busy* and, when time literally equated to money, certainly too busy for the time and creativity that a serious commitment to innovation required. And no one really knew what innovation *looked* like. Lawyers are not often heralded for their powers of imagination and so it was perhaps unsurprising they conspired to "innovation lite" – reduced rates, capped fee arrangements, use of low-cost solution providers, and automation of usual processes. Chapter four, by Jonathan Fortnam of Aston University Law School, explores the profoundly different environment for its people and its clients when innovation is founded on the alignment of financial, client, and people brand interests. Drawing on first-hand experience, Jonathan explores the difference an environment can make that is not only sympathetic to innovation but that drives and rewards it in transparent and mutually beneficial ways.

Recruiting talent from outside the industry can feel counterintuitive for legal practices, but there is a growing shift in attitude towards the appointment of non-lawyers to key business roles within law firms. Forward-thinking firms are increasingly using non-lawyer appointments to great effect. In chapter five, Neil Lloyd, managing director of FBC Manby Bowdler, discusses how the firm has created an operations board of people who are professionals in their own field to oversee the management of the business, giving a fresh perspective and generating new ideas that have unlocked many commercial and cultural benefits.

Disappointing financial results in law firms frequently (arguably, almost always) can be traced to problems in practice group performance. Business planning and financial management at the practice group level is the linchpin that connects the firm's business and strategic objectives to the people who have to achieve them. In chapter six, Norman K. Clark of Walker Clark LLC explains the essential elements of effective financial leadership of a practice group and how the factors that are most influential on sustainable profitability might vary significantly among practice groups, even in the same firm. Analysing the client base of the practice group, Norman considers how relentless and continuing attention to quality in practice group operations can lead to a new level of practice group financial management.

In chapter seven, Colin Jasper, principal at Positive Pricing, explains why pricing strategies cannot be developed at a firm level, and outlines essential elements of a practice group pricing strategy that contributes to the overall profitability of the practice.

Corporate clients frequently cite knowledge of their industry, business, and key issues they face as primary motivating factors in selecting (or deselecting) outside counsel. While many firms would say their practice groups are aligned to the industries of their clients, their knowledge of the minutiae of those industries – or sub-industries – may not be as complete as it needs to be. In chapter eight, Patrick J. McKenna, internationally recognized author, lecturer, strategist, and seasoned advisor to the leaders of premier professional service firms, provides some lessons on focusing your practice team around industry clients.

Without specific, achievable milestones set out, a practice will not be able to measure its progress – or otherwise – over time, and in line with the firm's overall objectives. Fittingly, therefore, the next chapter of this book examines this key piece of the leadership puzzle. John Sterling, founding partner of Sterling Strategies, LLC, describes the balanced scorecard framework for adopting implementation action plans and related measures that drive strategy implementation, and explains how this approach can be employed in a practice group context.

Finally, in chapter ten, lawyer, author and founder of Authentically Speaking, Hannah Beko explores how a coaching versus a managerial style can support practice group leaders to improve engagement, retention, and productivity inside their teams. The chapter includes coaching questions and reflection exercises for leaders to consider both for their own growth and development and for their group as a whole.

About the authors

Hannah Beko is a commercial property partner with challenger law firm gunner*cooke* llp. Outside her legal practice she runs coaching and training consultancy Authentically Speaking, specializing in supporting lawyers and law firms. After coaching and training thousands of lawyers, industry expert Hannah co-authored *Future-proof Your Legal Career: 10 Core Areas of Professional Development* (with Clare Jones and Steve Couch, published by Globe Law and Business in 2021) and is also a podcast host and a keynote speaker on mental health and wellbeing in the legal profession.

Norman K. Clark is the managing principal of the international legal management consultancy Walker Clark LLC, which he helped to found in 2002. His consulting practice specialises in issues of strategic planning and implementation, law firm profitability, governance, and quality assurance. His 48-year career as a lawyer includes experience as a trial lawyer, trial judge, law professor, and senior manager of the delivery of legal services on a global scale. He has been a full-time business adviser to the legal profession for the past 25 years, having advised clients in law firms, as well as corporate and government law departments, in more than 70 countries on five continents. Norman holds a BSc, a JD and an LLM. He is a retired member of the Pennsylvania Bar, a past Chair of the International Bar Association Law Firm Management Committee, and a past Co-Chair of the American Bar Association Cross-Border Practice Management Committee.

Jonathan Fortnam has been dean of Aston University Law School since September 2019. The Aston Law programs embrace not only the law of business but also the future of law and the business of law. Prior to his appointment at the University, Jonathan was for nearly 30 years a solicitor (including 21 as a partner) with international law firm Pinsent Masons LLP. During his time in practice, Jonathan led a number of client service teams whose work contributed to Pinsent Masons being acknowledged as

Law Firm of the Year in 2016 and 2019; as well as the FT's Innovative Law Firm of the Year in 2020. Jonathan was also joint winner of The Lawyer Business Leadership Award for innovation in financial management in 2016 and Legal Week's "Future of Legal Services Innovation" award in 2015.

Colin Jasper has consulted to professional services firms for over 25 years. During this time, he has had the opportunity to work with most of the leading law firms in the US, the UK, and Asia as well as leading accounting, engineering, and consulting firms. As one of the founding principals of Positive Pricing, Colin's focus is on assisting professional services firms to win more work, at higher prices, while improving client satisfaction. He has been a keynote speaker at conferences in the UK, the US, China, Singapore, Malaysia, and Australia. Colin's Legal Pricing Masterclasses have run since 2011. They have been delivered in Auckland, Boston, Chicago, Hong Kong, London, New York, San Francisco, Sydney, and Washington DC Pricing directors at many of the world's leading law firms have attended these programs. Colin was the director of the Business-to-Business Pricing program at the Australian Graduate School of Management. He has been a guest lecturer at numerous universities and business schools. Colin is the co-founder of the Legal Pricing Roundtables, a forum for those responsible for leading pricing within their firms. The Roundtables meet twice yearly in both New York and London. Colin's articles have been published in a range of journals and magazines including *Professional Services Firms Journal*, *The Law Management Journal*, and the *Journal of the Professional Pricing Society*. Colin has been recognized as the Legal Educator of the Year by the True Value Partnering Institute and has been inducted as a Fellow of the College of Law Practice Management for his contribution to pricing in the legal market.

Neil Lloyd is managing director of FBC Manby Bowdler. Ranked in both the *Legal 500* and *Chambers*, FBC Manby Bowdler is a 27-partner firm with over 170 staff working from six offices across the West Midlands, Shropshire and Worcestershire in the UK. Neil first joined FBC Manby Bowdler as sales director in 2015. Working closely with the wider support functions, Neil helped develop the firm's sales infrastructure to support the achievement of the company's overall business plan objectives and growth strategy. Neil is an affiliate of the IFS School of Finance and has been an associate of the Chartered Banker Institute since 2016.

Patrick J. McKenna is an internationally recognized author, lecturer, strategist, and seasoned advisor to the leaders of premier professional service firms, having had the honor of working with at least one of the largest firms in over a dozen different countries. He is the author of 12 books, most notably his international business bestseller, *First Among Equals*, currently in its sixth printing and translated into nine languages. His most recent work is *Industry Specialization: Making Competitors Irrelevant* (Legal Business World Publishing, 2022). Patrick's three decades of experience led to his being the subject of a Harvard Law School Case Study entitled *Innovations in Legal Consulting* (2011). One example of that innovation was his launching the first instructional program designed to specifically address the issues that new firm leaders of larger firms face in their First 100 Days – which graduated over 80 new leaders, many from AmLaw 100 and 200-sized law firms, as well as from notable accounting and consulting firms. Patrick serves as contributing editor to *Of Counsel, The Legal Practice and Management Report* based in New York; is the recipient of an "Honorary Fellowship" from Leaders Excellence of Harvard Square; and was voted by the readers of *Legal Business World Magazine* as one of only seven international thought leaders.

Susan Raridon Lambreth is a principal with LawVision Group. She has consulted to law firms for over 25 years. She is a noted author and specializes in practice group leadership and management and legal project management. She has written eight books on law firm management, including most recently, *Running Legal Like a Business* (with co-author Connie Brenton and published by Practising Law Institute), *The Power of Legal Project Management* (ABA, 2021), *Optimizing Practice Management: Driving Profitability and Market Position* (with co-author Wendy Bernero), Ark, 2015 and *The Practice Group Leader's Handbook for Success*.

Dr Larry Richard is recognized as the leading expert on the psychology of lawyer behavior. A former litigator, he earned a Ph.D. in Psychology at Temple University where he studied lawyers and law firms. He has advised dozens of AmLaw 200 law firms on leadership, management, and related issues such as teams, change management, talent selection, assessment, and other aspects of strategic talent management. Widely known as an expert on the lawyer personality, he has gathered personality data on thousands of lawyers. He is the founder and principal consultant at LawyerBrain LLC.

Michael Roster was formerly managing partner of Morrison & Foerster's Los Angeles office, co-chair of the firm's Financial Institutions Practice Group worldwide, resident in both LA and DC, and a member of the firm's policy committee. In 1993, Roster was appointed general counsel of Stanford University, Stanford Medical Center, and Stanford Management Company. He subsequently was executive vice president and general counsel of Golden West Financial Corporation. Michael has served as chair of the Association of Corporate Counsel, an outside director and vice chair of Silicon Valley Bank, chair of the Stanford Alumni Association, steering committee co-chair of ACC's Value Challenge, and chair of two start-up companies. He currently teaches Contract Drafting and Analysis at the University of Southern California Gould School of Law and is a director of MDRC in New York, a non-profit organization that evaluates the effectiveness of government and other programs affecting lower income families and individuals.

Susan Saltonstall Duncan is the founder and president of RainMaking Oasis and for nearly 40 years has provided management consulting and coaching services to law firms professional service organizations and individual professionals. She is the author of *Building Enduring Client Loyalty: A Guide for Lawyers and Their Firms* published by Globe Law and Business in 2021 and has authored numerous chapters on succession planning, women lawyers and executive presence, and other topics important to lawyer and law firm success. As a consultant, coach, and strategist, Susan works with firms, practice groups, and individual professionals on firm and practice/sector strategy, client relationship management and development, client feedback and needs assessment programs, business development training, coaching and strategy, succession planning, lateral integration strategies, firm values, visions, and culture and innovation.

Susan has served in in-house roles in large law firms including director of professional development, director of business development and as chief strategy officer for a Global 25 law firm. She was inducted as a Fellow in the College of Law Practice Management (COLPM) and into the Legal Marketing Association's Hall of Fame. She has widely published in legal publications, is regularly quoted in the press, and speaks for national and international associations.

John Sterling is chief strategy and practice development officer at Chapman and Cutler in Chicago. He has over 30 years' experience in the areas of strategic management and marketing. At Chapman he is responsible for strategy development and implementation at the firm, practice group, and individual levels. John brings extensive law firm strategy and marketing experience to this publication, along with a background helping corporations with strategic planning, marketing planning, and market research. That experience includes strategic management, market research, and market planning assignments for dozens of law firms and/or their respective practice groups. He is the author of two books on law firm strategic planning and strategy implementation (via balanced scorecards). John is a past president of the Association for Strategic Planning – Chicago chapter. He was president of the Strategic Management Association in Chicago and the Strategic Leadership Forum. He is also a contributing editor to *Strategy & Leadership*, a leading strategic management journal. Prior to joining Chapman and Cutler, John was CMO for Sterne Kessler Goldstein & Fox, a founding partner of Sterling Strategies and of Smock*Sterling Strategic Management Consultants, was a senior consultant with Ernst & Young's Great Lakes Strategic Management and Marketing Group, and was a senior policy analyst at the University of Illinois at Chicago.

Chapter 1:
Role and responsibilities of practice group leaders

By Susan Saltonstall Duncan, president, RainMaking Oasis

Introduction

Practice groups in law firms most often operate as important "business units" within a firm's broader departmental structure. It is often at the practice group level that firms do their budgeting and revenue tracking, hiring and training, business development, and marketing. This has made the role of practice group leader increasingly important, but also much more challenging to do well.

There are a number of important functions that practice group leaders must engender and oversee:

- Coordination, communication and accountability of team members;
- Creating a sense of belonging, team collaboration;
- Innovation and collective brainstorming;
- Optimal client service and delivery as measured through client feedback;
- Knowledge building and sharing;
- Development and dissemination of skills and expertise;
- Utilization and development of associates;
- Marketing and external market focus;
- Strong brand and reputation; and
- Improved financial management and profitability.

Given the importance practice groups play in firms, those who lead these practice groups play a critical role in the efficient and effective delivery of services to clients and to the growth and profitability of the firm. Effective practice group leaders wear many hats, including that of strategist, financial expert, operations specialist, practice expert, coach, disciplinarian, and cheerleader. Few practice group leaders will excel in all areas, to say nothing of having to balance this role with building and maintaining a productive practice and client base of one's own.

This chapter sets the stage for the role and responsibilities of effective practice group leaders, including:

- General traits and skills of practice group leaders;
- Practice group leader as strategist, including developing and executing a practice group plan;
- Practice group leader as financial steward, including areas of financial performance oversight;
- Practice group leader as talent manager and coach; and
- Steps to accelerate practice group leader effectiveness.

Attributes that make effective practice group leaders

Many of today's practice group leaders were selected for their abilities as top rainmakers and producers. While effective leaders share a few traits embodied by successful rainmakers – such as discipline, drive, good listening, empathy and resilience – rainmakers most often use these attributes best in the context of client expansion, client development, and new business origination and sales. Rainmakers are often less inclined to use these traits when leading colleagues and staff and managing internal business. Unfortunately, there are partners who insist on having the role of practice group leader either for status or control, despite not having the skills, interest, or willingness to devote the time to do the job well.

Perhaps one of the most important aspects of being a practice group leader is creating a team that collaborates and communicates and where individual members routinely commit time and energy to advancing the team's objectives. In law firms, where partners prize and protect their autonomy and can often be more focused on their own progress, agendas, and rewards, this is a particularly challenging aspect of the job.

Traits and skills of effective practice group leaders include:

- Puts interests of practice group and firm above own and treats as leadership role as a top priority;
- Willing and able to devote necessary time to do a good job;
- Authority to make decisions quickly and implement effectively;
- Commitment to improve the firm's long-term stability, profitability, and productivity;

- Understanding of the firm, its goals and philosophy, and its need for administrative management;
- Strong organization; able to prioritize issues and tasks and delegate where feasible;
- Good listening, facilitation, and mediation skills;
- Understand the needs of people and the nuances of issues;
- Generates respect from other partners as a practitioner, leader, and fair individual;
- Willing and able to confront peers, take a position, hold others accountable; and
- Takes responsibility for decisions and holds self accountable.

Practice group leader as strategist

It is surprising how many law firms, their leaders, and partners eschew the discipline of planning and strategy. Many firms still do not require annual business plans or even the process of planning from their partners or practice groups and many don't even have a strategic plan for the firm. Law firm partners and even leaders often believe that creating plans is a waste of time, because things happen quickly and change constantly. They might even share stories of how their best client or new area of expertise was developed serendipitously and opportunistically.

In order for practice groups to effectively execute client and growth strategies, it is necessary to execute a disciplined and intentional approach to planning and implementation that incorporates client and competitive market intelligence and is aligned with firm strategy. A practice group leader should drive the planning process that includes the following components:

- Internal and external analysis;
- SWOT/gap analysis;
- Client service feedback, marketing, and business development;
- Innovation around delivery, staffing, packing, and pricing;
- Talent management including laterals, general hiring, training and development, retention, diversity;
- Client/partner succession; and
- Development and execution of annual, measurable goals and a plan.

Step 1: Internal practice analysis

This first step in the planning process focuses primarily on an internal assessment of the skills, areas of expertise, depth and breadth of talent, staffing and delivery of services, and overall strengths and weaknesses of the practice group. Specific areas of analysis often include:

- Skills inventory and core capabilities analysis: current technical knowledge/skill sets, range/depth of services and experience, technical expertise and experience gaps in segments, gaps in skills or staffing.
- Innovation and service delivery review: project management, process improvement, staffing models, efficiencies, tracking of metrics, knowledge repositories, and the use of automation/technology and allied service providers, new products.
- Practice management analysis: internal organization and policies, work assignment and staffing, training and supervision, knowledge management and technology, quality control, new matter/client intake, team collaboration.
- Client relationships, satisfaction, and expansion: relationship history, relationship matrix, three-year revenue trends of practice group for its top 50 practice group clients, share of clients' legal spend, exported revenue (clients/matters sent to other practice groups of the firm), revenue by clusters (industry, geographic, issue/subspecialty), lost or dissatisfied clients, client feedback and retention, cross-selling and co-marketing involvement with other practice groups (PGs) or or interdisciplinary teams.
- Profitability and financial performance analysis: revenues, write-offs, realization and collection time, billing rates and pricing models, timekeeper utilization and leverage, profitability by service/matter type, and overall profit margin of types of work/clients.
- Marketing and business development effectiveness: sources of business, prospect pipeline tracking, RFP and pitch process, referral sources, successes/failures, branding/positioning, industry and business conferences, events and sponsorships, entertainment, support, strengths and weaknesses, and ROI.
- Cross-practice opportunities: other PGs that routinely refer work, industry groups, cross-specialty practice services and opportunities.
- Talent and succession: hiring, including lateral hiring and integration, retention, training and development, work assignment

and oversight, diversity, retention, employee engagement, succession, and retirement.

- Practice group governance and management: leadership effectiveness (360 reviews), communication and engagement, conflict resolution, new client intake, and conflicts and quality control.
- Practice group member input: a survey and interviews/focus groups to gather input on threats, opportunities, strengths and weaknesses of PG.

Step 2: External market and trend research

Following trends and market developments, gauging clients' needs, and tracking competitors is vital to designing and executing successful strategies. The following components should be undertaken:

- Market and trend analysis: service demand trends, geographic markets, client industries and segments, economic, political, social and demographic, legislative and regulatory trends, market and industry opportunities and threats, and technology trends.
- Client needs and market perception analysis: surveys and interviews with clients and other business leaders, trends reports by Big Four and management consulting firms, client and prospect needs, preferences and purchasing behaviors including whether legal spend is growing or shrinking, and percentage of client legal spend the practice group currently receives.
- Competitive analysis: key competitors the practice group regularly encounters in cases, deals, client pitches, and conference sponsorships, including alternative legal service providers and technology platforms, market share and growth, perceived image and performance, current positioning, pricing and marketing strategies.
- Opportunity analysis: new products/services, new geographic and industry markets, new legislation/regulation/case law, niches, all in alignment with current and future client needs.

Step 3: SWOT analysis, visioning, and goal-setting

Once the data collection, research, and analysis have been completed, a summary should be shared at a minimum with all partners in the practice group, and ideally with associates and other professionals in the group. The practice group, or a representative subgroup, should meet to discuss the full findings. The SWOT summarizes the Strengths (internal, firm focused), Weaknesses (internal, firm focused), Opportunities (external, market-focused), and Threats (external, market-focused) in an easily digestible box format. The group may want to (re)define its "ideal client", "ideal services", and "ideal industries/markets" profiles based on its top clients, profitability assessment, market trends, and opportunities and service strengths.

Once that is discussed, the next step is to craft a Vision Statement for the practice group – this is an aspirational, inspirational, and achievable summary of the practice group's view of itself in the future and the outcomes and benefits it strives for. After the vision, the group must determine measurable goals for the practice group for the next year. These goals will be what drives the action plan that is then developed and will usually include financial, practice, client development, and marketing goals.

Step 4: Devise and execute a 12-month business plan

The business plan should be formatted as a working document (not in memo form!) so that deadlines, person(s) responsible and budgets can be attached to specific objectives and action items and updated at least on a quarterly basis. Goals should be measurable, quantifiable, and specific. Most practice group plans will incorporate several key areas of strategy:

- Growth: laterals, new markets, new services/niches, new clients;
- Revenue/budget and profitability;
- Client service, delivery, and satisfaction;
- Innovation, delivery, and pricing;
- Business development and marketing, including cross-selling and cross-practice marketing; and
- Succession transitions.

In many firms, practice group leaders draft the practice group plan, usually but not always with some input from a few partners. A better way is to have several partners and even associates involved in the assessment activities and all members involved in the development of goals and an action plan. If the practice group is very large (more than 20 lawyers) you likely will need to operate with sub-specialties. The planning process can be broken into smaller groups and then brought together at the end. In order for your plan to be effectively executed, all practice group members will have to feel invested, take ownership, and be assigned responsibilities, and then held accountable for the completion of tasks.

Practice groups should meet on a regular basis, at least monthly, with a structured agenda, to review progress against the plan, and to update it with any new opportunities. Some groups find it easier to keep a running action list that is updated after every meeting rather than keeping the original plan updated every month, but it is important to use the goals and plan to identify priority agenda items for each meeting. Ideally, all practice groups in a firm should follow the same model of pre-plan assessment and a template for their actual plans. This allows practice group leaders and firm management to share other practice groups' plans, regularly monitor progress against goals, and easily identify areas for synergy or opportunity.

Practice group leader as financial steward

As firms continue to grow in size and complexity, it is often no longer possible for them to drive, manage, and measure the revenue growth of the firm only through the central leadership. The concept of practice groups operating as business units is that they now have primary responsibility for overseeing major aspects of their firm's financial health. Practice groups are usually the vehicles through which firms develop their annual revenue projections and expense budgets and help manage the risks inherent in a professional practice. While fluctuations can occur, sound financial management has become a key responsibility of practice groups and the partners who lead them.

This is a major responsibility for practice group leaders and is another reason that most larger groups have co-leaders or a deputy. There is often a division of responsibilities and the financial stewardship resides with one of them. Large practice groups often have business operations directors who help monitor and report on financial performance. Fortunately, there are numerous technology tools that effectively track the various performance metrics and can provide real time data on individual timekeeper numbers, and aggregate group numbers. This prevents surprises from occurring and allows practice group leaders to address and make course corrections in real time. Many of these tools are also accessible to partners so they can track their own productivity metrics against goals.

Areas of financial performance oversight

There are several areas of financial performance and related risks that practice group leaders are responsible for:

- Risk management: client intake and work acceptance standards, identification of clients and matters that pose the greatest risk, sound quality control practices such as "second" lawyering, new matter intake, conflicts, time-keeping, billing, rates, alternative fee arrangements, collections and write-offs.
- Productivity: ongoing monitoring of number of timekeepers, utilization, workloads, billing rates, leverage, bottlenecks, project scoping, resource allocation and efficient project management, monitoring and underperformance.
- Annual revenue budget: projected net revenue based on hours and collections, other streams (premium/bonus fees, contingency billing, etc.) minus discounts, write-offs.
- Annual expense budget: in addition to practice groups' overhead allotment and personnel and staffing ratios, practice groups must track travel, marketing, client development, sponsorships, business development, and entertainment expenses; this might also include lateral hiring expenses and continuing legal education costs.
- Pricing: hourly rates, alternative fee arrangements including flat fees, capped fees, premium billing, hold-backs with success fee, and contingency.
- Revenue and financial metrics: fee growth, realization, utilization, leverage, matter profitability, timesheet write-offs/write-downs, fee/price discounts, unbilled work in progress (WIP), and accounts receivable/weeks carried before collected. Another important metric to analyze is revenue leakage, which happens when time is recorded but not billed, discounted, time is written-off, or there are long gaps in billing and collections.
- Success metrics: in addition to monitoring the statistics, many practice group leaders now establish metrics that can easily be measured on a quarterly basis that reflect growth in revenue and increased productivity and profitability. Some are less directly a financial metric but still reflect improvement in areas that often lead to new business. Examples include:
  - Increased revenue into practice from new clients;
  - Increased revenue per lawyer;
  - Increased realization for PG;

  - Increased utilization per lawyer;
  - Increased profitability of matters;
  - Increased revenue into PG from other PGs;
  - Increased referrals and revenue to other PGs;
  - Number of client meetings;
  - Number of prospect meetings;
  - Number of referrals; and
  - Number of proposals and pitches.
- Key performance indicators: in addition to success metrics listed previously, other aspects of financial and service performance will be important to track and measure on a regular basis. Examples include top clients, changes in top clients, active clients from year to year and dollar value, inactive or lost clients, average fee, and number of matters per client.

Practice group leader as talent manager and coach

Perhaps one of the most challenging responsibilities for today's practice group leaders is the "people" side of the business. While practice group leaders often get help from others managing the associates and staff in the practice groups, they are increasingly spending time and energy meeting with partners, running interference, resolving disputes, and providing support and encouragement. It can be time-consuming and energy draining.

This aspect of practice group leadership is perhaps the most important, but it is not a skill set many practice group leaders possess, especially those who landed the position by virtue of their success as a rainmaker and large books of business. As a result, firms are either providing skills training to practice group leaders and/or selecting new, co- or deputy leaders who can serve as coaches, motivators, mediators, communicators, and morale-builders.

Coach

Practice group leaders are expected to have genuine concern for everyone on their team, but especially for their partners' personal wellbeing, professional development, and success. This requires practice group leaders to get to know all members of the practice group – what their goals are and what motivates them. They should speak with and meet with each partner every four to six months, including annual visits to those in other offices, to review the status of their personal business plans and to discuss workloads, matters, business development, operational issues, mentoring and talent management, and practice development.

Effective practice group leaders are accessible and have an open-door policy. They provide ongoing and constructive feedback and are empathetic listeners. As a coach, practice group leaders encourage partners and others to take risks, to think creatively and innovatively, and will support them if their efforts fail. Leaders also have to hold partners accountable to ensure they meet or exceed goals and expectations and may have to address disruptive behaviors on the part of some partners.

Communicator and collaborator

Practice group leaders must understand and work effectively with different communications styles and personalities. They need to establish open lines of communication with members of the practice group by holding effective monthly practice group meetings that encourage participation and commitment from all levels of timekeeper and staff, communicating about practice group and firm matters, trends, new clients, etc.

As firms continue to get larger, many lawyers and staff get frustrated with a lack of transparency and knowledge about what is going on in the firm. Effective practice group leaders share information and updates on firm strategy, new policies, and on anything else that is likely to impact others' practice development or operational effectiveness. Practice group leaders should also actively participate in meetings with other practice group leaders to share best practices and strategize about challenges they're having, as well as look for opportunities for cross-selling.

Motivator, morale-, and team-builder

Practice group leaders set the tone for a positive work environment that expects, encourages, and celebrates collaboration within the practice group and with others in and across the firm. As leaders, they are responsible for establishing a vision and ground rules for the PG, having sought input from others to do so. Practice group leaders should push people to do their best and take pride in their work and their teams and be generous with credit and celebrating successes.

Talent manager

Finally, there is a fair amount of time spent on assessing what is needed at every level of service delivery – the skills, experience, seniority level, and non-traditional expertise. Practice group leaders continually monitor workloads and client demands and anticipate in advance where either understaffing or overstaffing is likely to occur. In concert with other firm professionals and in alignment with firm goals, practice group leaders will oversee:

- Recruiting for associates and other timekeepers to include consideration of increasing diversity and the changing nature of the workforce and working model;
- Diversity and inclusion considerations;
- Lateral partners – due diligence, conflict and profitability analyses, recruiting and negotiation process, successful integration, and monitoring performance progress at six-month intervals;
- Associate mentoring, training, CLE, training benchmarks and checklists, and other professional development resources;
- Attorney retention, which has become particularly challenging given the changing and flexible work options introduced during the COVID-19 pandemic;
- Performance and compensation reviews; and
- Succession and retirement of senior partners, selection/coaching of successors, and ensuring the next generation is ready to assume responsibilities.

Ways to accelerate practice group leader effectiveness

There are a number of steps that law firms can take to improve the skills, performance, and commitment of partners who serve in the role of practice group leader.

1. Define the roles and responsibilities of the practice group leader job and write a job description; include a description of how the leader will be evaluated, measured and compensated. Share this with partners in advance to ensure they understand them and agree to them.
2. Put the right leaders into the position by formally assessing partners' personality traits before appointing them practice group leader, using the defined objectives of the practice group and the likely responsibilities and traits to identify ideal candidates.
3. Reward and recognize leaders through compensation and public

recognition; compensate them for their substantial time commitment and provide relief from ambitious client/billable goal requirements.

4. Hold leaders accountable for executing their responsibilities through regular reporting.
5. Provide training in all of the core responsibility areas such as finance, project management, knowledge management, coaching, business planning, business development, performance review, team-building, communications, including addressing conflict and having difficult conversations, emotional intelligence, and time management.
6. Inculcate an emotional intelligence culture that lends itself to successful leadership – 360-degree reviews, personality assessments, sharing and application of findings, teamwork.
7. Provide them with their own executive coach who can serve as a sounding board.
8. Schedule quarterly one-on-one meetings/calls with the managing partner to share progress, feedback, strategic and operational priority shifts.
9. Develop a team-coaching forum for all practice group leaders to meet at least quarterly to share challenges and success strategies.
10. Provide dedicated, professional support via a business manager, a business development manager, and/or a skilled and organized executive assistant (who isn't assigned to two to five other partners/lawyers!).
11. Ask the partner to complete a self-assessment on a semi-annual basis to be shared and discussed with the firm's managing partner (or department chair).
12. Begin training the next generation of practice group leaders early on, either by giving them a role as a deputy leader and/or through distributive leadership, whereby younger partners in the practice group are given discrete areas of responsibility, e.g., hiring, associate reviews and development, marketing, etc.

Chapter 2: **The practice group leader as change agent**

By Susan Raridon Lambreth, principal, LawVision Group, and Dr Larry Richard, founder and principal consultant, LawyerBrain LLC

Practice group leaders are among the most essential players in achieving a law firm's long-term success. They help the group's lawyers set and achieve well-defined goals related to strategy, market position, talent acquisition and development, firm culture, and profitability.

In a time of accelerating change, like we're experiencing today, the PGL must serve an even more vital role – the role of change agent. A change agent is, in essence, an effective leader. Research at Harvard has shown that in times of great change, the people within an organization express a greater need for leadership.[1] Leadership is a response to external change and uncertainty. Change agents cope with impending external change by initiating internal change, and by leading their constituents to move in the new direction.

But can lawyers, particularly practice group leaders, step into the change agent role? There are a number of barriers that must be overcome first.

A *Forbes* magazine article from 2014 had the title, "Every leader must be a change agent or face extinction".[2] Unfortunately, few PGLs think of themselves as change agents or understand their role in that way. This is a problem, because a "change agent" mindset is a critical element of success in these roles. Coping with change is challenging enough in any business organization. But law firms have added at least two hurdles that are absent in most other businesses. First, the nature of law practice requires lawyers to hunt for problems and to be suspicious and vigilant in dealing with others, in order to protect their clients. This responsibility, and the training that equips lawyers to carry it out, breeds a very change-averse and risk-averse outlook. Moreover, research by one of the authors into the personality traits of lawyers[3] shows over and over again that individuals who enter and succeed in the legal profession have disproportionately high levels of skepticism compared to the general public. This personality trait strengthens and reinforces the outlook cultivated by their training, thus imposing not one but two layers of skepticism, change aversion, and risk aversion.

Further compounding these challenges is the fact that law firms are "owner"-run businesses with a small number of the top business producers essentially controlling the decision-making in many firms. And, in many instances, these top producers do not want the firm to change as it may affect their current position, autonomy, or earnings. In the 2020 Altman Weil survey, "Law Firms in Transition,"[4] 65 percent of leaders surveyed reported that the reason they do not implement more change efforts in their organizations, despite client pressures and market imperatives, is because "partners resist most change efforts".

Another issue affecting the ability of law firm leaders to effect change in their organizations is the insecurity many lawyers feel today in response to the tremendous change occurring across the profession. In the late 1990s, while leading a PGL training workshop, our co-presenter from Harvard turned to the group of PGLs from various firms and said:

> *"It is a myth you can't teach old dogs new tricks. The research now shows you can teach people way into their eighties. What you can't do is teach 'scared dogs' new tricks."*

A light bulb went on as we were seeing lots of "scared dog" lawyers in our practice – almost paralyzed from the rapid change that was going on in the legal field at the time as technology was rapidly changing and the "dot.com" boom was happening. Today, the pace of change is much faster, particularly since the beginning of the COVID-19 pandemic. There are many more "scared lawyers" in the practice groups that PGLs are trying to lead. Not recognizing this, i.e. approaching change in a way that turns a blind eye to uncertainty and lawyer insecurity, dooms change efforts to fail.

As if all of the above weren't enough to make it challenging to turn lawyers into leaders, the exponential increase in uncertainty, anxiety, and mental health impact from the pandemic has raised the stakes even higher. All human beings have a threat-sensing circuit in our brains designed to detect situations that might harm us. Uncertainty triggers this circuit, and unending uncertainty like we've been experiencing can lead to a constant state of distractibility, irritability, anxiety, and passivity. Practice group leaders need to understand this dynamic – at least some of the rudimentary neuroscience underpinnings as well as the practical consequences – because no leader can be effective if they don't understand the role these forces play and the tools at their disposal to mitigate them.

What does it mean to be a change agent in your role as a PGL?
First, a change agent by definition has just two primary tasks:

1. Setting a new direction, despite the fact that there is insufficient information to be entirely sure that it's the right direction; and
2. Mobilizing his/her constituents to move in that direction.

Setting a direction can be challenging enough, but most lawyers, because of their high intelligence and strong analytical abilities, are able to identify possible goals and general direction fairly readily. Mobilizing other lawyers to follow their lead, however, is a road littered with obstacles.

The biggest enemy of every change agent is the complacency of the lawyers. Practice groups that have experienced success in achieving their goals despite or even because of the changing environment are the most vulnerable to this kind of complacency. In today's climate, every PGL in every firm should be thinking seriously about these issues, even if – or especially if – your practice group has had many years of strong profitability and growth.

Law firms that were successful just a few years ago are folding or merging to survive today. New competitors for all levels of legal work are entering the market daily. Over $1 billion is invested in new legal start-ups almost every year.[5] If a PGL does not keep his/her group moving forward and changing to be relevant in the market, the group runs a strong risk of losing market share and declining. Thus, the number one mission of a PGL-as-change-agent is to embrace change. This is a "mindset" first, and a behavior second. PGLs must err on the side of believing that "change" is a realistic threat, and that anticipating change and taking bold action to prepare for it is vital.

What else does a PGL need to be a change agent?
First, across the business world, common characteristics of change agents include:

- Clear vision;
- Ability to inspire;
- Ability to experiment;
- Role modeling/leading by example;
- Building trust relationships;
- Patience and persistence;

- Resilience; and
- A servant-leader mindset.

Each important characteristic is described below, with advice on how you can implement or work on each one.

Clear vision and focus

Research and common sense both tell us that people are more likely to follow a leader when the leader presents a clear vision for the goal, and helps people understand the implications of reaching that goal. The best goals employ both the "carrot" and the "stick". The "stick" – building a sense of urgency, the imperative for change, the reasons why the status quo is no longer working – mobilizes people to want to change. But the stick alone is insufficient to sustain behavior change. A "carrot" is also needed. Carrots work best when they're inspirational, when people derive meaning from them. So a PGL needs to craft both elements of the vision. The PGL does not have to know all the details of how the practice group should implement its goals without input from the group's members, but PGLs should have at least a broad vision of where they want to take the group. Many groups have a business plan and that is an important part of driving buy-in and change in the group. But, even without a formal plan or before one is developed, the PGL should have a vision of some strategic priorities that are critical for the group:

- Is the primary area for improvement the group's market position or brand?
- Does the group need to change its practice mix and move away from some types of less profitable work?
- Does the group need to recruit talent to replace rainmakers or senior lawyers with great knowledge that will be retiring in the next five years?
- Does the group need to enhance engagement of its members and develop greater cohesion and "glue" in the group?
- Is the group attractive to younger professionals so they will want to join the group and work hard enough and long enough to make partner?

Having at least a general sense of the vision of the firm over the next two to three years is critical and should drive the way the PGL spends his time.

If the PGL does not have even a general sense of vision for the group, they should be interviewing clients and looking at competitive intelligence to begin to develop it. Also, because many lawyers tend to be more focused on details than the big picture, a PGL may need to get input from more visionary lawyers in or outside the practice group and other business professionals in the firm to help shape or flesh out the vision for the group.

In addition to the broad vision that is like an overarching umbrella of what the group should focus on, the PGL should lead the group in the development of a strategic business plan. While some firms or groups have become frustrated with annual business planning processes or feel that these plans are not worthwhile, it is often a function of flaws in the planning process. Too many PGLs do not understand how to achieve partner buy-in through the planning process – which is as important as the plan itself. One of the most important elements to achieve high levels of group performance is common goals shared by group members. The planning process is often the best way to develop these. This process is invaluable in:

1. Developing a shared view of the market, which should drive the need to move forward and make changes (thereby shaking some complacency that often prevents actions to change);
2. Engaging group members to own the goals and action steps so they are willing to spend time implementing the plan and effecting change; and
3. Developing a small number of priority goals.

The PGL needs to push the group to have no more than two or three goals, as the latest research shows having more than three goals reduces the likelihood of achieving any of them.[6] Pushing the group to focus and prioritize, rather than compromise with long lists of goals so everyone is happy, is a critical role for the PGL.

Ability to inspire

It is not enough to just come up with an inspiring vision. PGLs need to be psychologically savvy. They need to understand how to mobilize, motivate, and otherwise move others to action. This requires emotional intelligence skills. The comfort zone for most lawyers is the skillful use of the intellect, which is certainly an asset in goal formation. But intellect alone is not enough. PGLs need to understand how to harness human emotions through the use of authenticity, face time, and an ability to accurately identify aspirational goals that touch others at a deep level. Mere rhetorical skills that may work well in a motion for summary judgment will not be sufficient to spur partners to take action in pursuit of a vision.

Ability to experiment

No one will be inspired by a vision that consists of incremental efforts to continue the status quo. By definition, leaders in a time of change are trying to take control in a world where the lack of predictability makes complete control impossible. Thus PGLs must innovate, take risks, and be willing to go in new directions.

Role modeling and leading by example

Practice group leaders cannot get others to change or do things if they are not role modeling those behaviors. The PGL cannot preach about the need to improve profitability and be one of the offenders on policies about not discounting, getting bills out promptly, or daily time entry. PGLs need to commit significant amounts of investment time (quality "non-billable" time) to build the group, just as they need other group members to spend investment time on it, in addition to their personal practice building. Practice group success today requires many members of the group investing time in client relationship management, mentoring and other engagement with junior professionals, legal project management, business development, professional development, knowledge management, and more. Getting outside their comfort zone to do these things shows others in the group both the importance of them and that they are achievable and realistic to accomplish. In addition, role modeling matters psychologically. Humans are hard-wired to follow leaders. When leaders walk their talk, others will follow; and when leaders don't walk their talk, others will follow.

Building trust relationships

It is critical that the PGL builds trust relationships with each member of the group. Trust relationships are critical to getting lawyers to buy-in and be part of moving the group forward, to sharing and collaborating and more. Without trust, the group will not function as a group but will exist as a confederation of individual practitioners. Even if the PGL has been close friends with some members of the group outside of work prior to taking on the group leadership role, typically they have not previously been involved in knowing the day-to-day practice of their colleagues in the group. And, it is hard for highly skeptical, low sociability lawyers to build trust with their colleagues. However, the PGL needs to learn about the practices and career aspirations for each partner at least (and all lawyers in smaller practice groups). This means knowing what type of work they are doing now, what they enjoy most or find most challenging, and where they would like to take their practice in the next few years. It means knowing the "pain points" or concerns about their practice in the current turbulent market for legal services. The old adage that a person "does not care how much you know until they know how much you care" actually applies here and showing you understand (and care about) your colleagues' practices, goals, aspirations, and needs goes a long way to build trust with them. A good, time-tested model for building trust is Stephen Covey's idea of the "Emotional Bank Account". In his book *The Seven Habits of Highly Effective People*,[7] Covey explains how certain behaviors, like keeping your word or not talking about others behind their backs, act like "deposits" to a bank account, and opposite behaviors, like constantly disappointing others or gossiping behind their backs, act like "withdrawals". Covey makes the point that one withdrawal can require many deposits to restore the status quo trust level.

Patience and persistence

Anyone in leadership in a law firm knows that change does not happen quickly and trying to force it only results in greater skepticism and resistance. The PGL needs to recognize the delicate balance required in pushing partners and others out of their complacency. If you share too much information about competitors, threats to the business, and more in order to overcome their complacency, you can cause your colleagues to want to leave for another firm or feel like they can't handle it and want to "sweep it under the carpet" – i.e. they stick their heads in the sand. On the other hand, if you don't push hard enough, and if all they hear are positive messages about how well the group is doing, it only reinforces their complacency and they will likely not see any need to change. The famous Chinese proverb fits here: *"To whom the gods wish to destroy, they send 40 years of success"*.

A PGL is often out ahead of his group members, seeing the market trends and other factors that the group needs to address to continue to be successful. But, if these are raised in a dramatic or dire way, the PGL will be viewed like "Chicken Little".[8] Instead, the PGL can be effective over time by working competitive intelligence, client quotes, and market data into each monthly practice group meeting, circulating articles or blog posts, and in other ways slowly sharing information that shows the group members "business as usual is not sustainable" so to prepare them for thinking about change. This takes patience as the PGL often recognizes the urgency for the changes, but also persistence as pushing too hard and fast can increase the number of "scared dogs" in the group and can reduce their trust in the PGL. When the typical law firm practice group is performing at very high levels and partners are making way more compensation than they ever expected when they graduated law school, it can seem irrational to raise warning signals. At the same time, any PGL monitoring the market and internal data can see the cracks in the seams that, if not addressed, could mean serious issues down the road for the practice group and its members.

Resilience

Research over the past 23 years by one of the authors shows a remarkable finding[9] – lawyers have the lowest levels of psychological resilience of any professional group. Resilience is a personality trait that refers to how one responds in the face of criticism, rejection, or other life setbacks. High resilience people do two things well in the face of adversity:

1. They tolerate life's bumps in the sense that they "roll with the punches" and don't let adverse events (criticism, rejection, etc.) knock them off their game.
2. When they do experience a setback (we all do at some point), they bounce back quicker and more adroitly than low resilience people do.

Dr Richard's statistics show that 90 percent of all lawyers tested score in the bottom half of the resilience scale. This finding has remained stable for the past 23 years. Low resilience people react to criticism or rejection defensively. They spend a lot of time providing defensive explanations for their behavior; they may avoid or deflect criticism; they may try to delay any conversation about their shortcomings; and they may counter-attack the person who criticizes or rejects them.

Low resilience is a challenge for most lawyers but it is a more important challenge for lawyers in leadership roles, like PGLs. We know that leaders naturally get criticized more than others – it comes with the territory. But we also know that when a criticized leader reacts defensively, that leader will lose credibility and followership from his or her constituents. Luckily, resilience is only partly dispositional (genetic). To a large extent, an individual can learn to become more resilient.

Unfortunately, lawyers have a harder time learning to be resilient than do people in other professions. This is because resilience is sensitive to two other factors, neither of which work in a lawyer's favor. First, individuals who are "optimistic" tend to be more resilient. "Optimistic" is used here not in the colloquial sense of seeing the world through rose-colored glasses, but in the more scientific sense of habitually favoring more positive explanations rather than negative ones when adversity strikes.[10] Second, individuals with strong, ongoing, authentic social connections tend to be higher in resilience in both senses of the word – they tolerate life's bumps better, and they bounce back quicker and more effectively when they hit a bump.

How do lawyers fare on these two resilience-boosters? Lousy! Our data show that lawyers are highly skeptical and pessimistic (skepticism's first cousin). They are constantly reinforced in their skeptical thinking, and this takes an ongoing toll on their resilience. In addition, our data show that lawyers are very low in a trait called "sociability", which measures one's inclination to authentically connect with others. Lawyers tend to be uncomfortable around intimacy, initiating authentic connections with others, being emotionally vulnerable, or even talking about relationships in general. The scientific evidence is piling up in favor of the critical importance of friendships, authentic connections, and other ongoing forms of emotional connections. Strong social connections have been linked to overall levels of life satisfaction, work satisfaction, relationship satisfaction, and even to longevity and one's general health profile and immune response. The atypically low levels of interest and skills in the relationship arena possessed by the majority of lawyers continues to hurt them, at the very least by depriving them of a formidable resilience-building factor.

Because of their high skepticism/pessimistic thinking and low sociability, it's harder for lawyers to maintain high resilience, and harder for them to learn how to build it up. But luckily it's not impossible. The experience of the authors shows that lawyers can readily learn resilience skills, and by doing so, they can make a pronounced and positive impact on their own life experience in very visible ways. This is an effort that every PGL should consider because low-resilience leaders have a very hard time retaining enthusiastic followers, while high-resilience leaders are far better equipped for the role. It is even more important today for leaders to work on their resilience in the uncertainty of the global pandemic that has plagued the globe for two years. More resilient leaders can help their group members build resilience.

Servant-leader mindset

In our research for the books we have written on practice group management,[11] the most effective PGLs interviewed always mention an important characteristic for success: the mindset of a servant-leader. They describe getting a high level of intrinsic motivation by seeing others succeed, more than just themselves – by seeing the whole group succeed, more than just their personal practice. It takes someone with this mindset to be willing to take the personal risks to push the group forward. The PGL needs to be a change agent – pushing the group through change even when many lawyers who are very successful in the current law firm model resist it. The key is a mindset that places the most importance on seeing the organization's success as primary and the practice group's success as nearly as important, placing their own interest off the radar screen. A PGL that is seen as self-serving is not trusted, which means other group members likely will not be willing to make changes they perceive as sacrifices or out of their comfort zone.

Benefits of being a change agent

A PGL that embraces this role as change agent not only enjoys the role more and is viewed as more effective, they see other benefits to the firm and their group. These include:

- Long-term viability and profitability of your practice group – having a shared vision, strategic goals, and better group cohesion through the steps above, the practice group is typically more viable and more profitable – and much more fun to be part of.
- Reduced lawyer attrition and enhanced morale – when a PGL functions as described above (creating a practice group focused on the future, engaging the members, building trust and more), the lawyers report a more enjoyable workplace, higher morale, and greater cohesion and commitment to the group. In today's "war for talent" amidst the "great resignation" of 2021/22, attracting and retaining your talent is seen as the most critical objective in most firms. Many firms have more work than they can handle and cannot afford high levels of attrition.

While it can push lawyer-leaders outside their comfort zone to be a change agent, the benefits both individually and for the group make it worth it.

References

1. John Kotter, *What Leaders Really Do.*
2. Llopis, G. "Every leader must be a change agent or face extinction," *Forbes*, 24 March 2014.
3. Skepticism is not the only outlier trait that characterizes lawyers. Dr Larry Richard's research also shows that the typical lawyer has a much higher than average tendency toward autonomy, urgency (impatience), and abstract reasoning (love of problem-solving and analytical thinking), and a much lower than average tendency toward sociability (lawyers are private and uncomfortable around relationship-based issues), and resilience (lawyers tend to be quite thin-skinned and defensive in the face of criticism or rejection). All of these traits have the potential to undercut effective leadership as well as effective coping with change.
4. www.altmanweil.com/LFit2020
5. https://news.crunchbase.com/news/legal-tech-venture-investment
6. McChesney, C., Huling, J., and Covey, S., *The Four Disciplines of Execution.*
7. Covey, S. *Seven Habits of Highly Effective People* (1989).
8. A European folk tale with a moral in the form of a chicken who believes that the world is coming to an end. The phrase "The sky is falling!" features prominently in the story and has passed into the English language as a common idiom indicating a hysterical or mistaken belief that disaster is imminent.
9. http://lawyerbrain.com/sites/default/files/leadership_in_law_firms_by_lrr_ark_group.pdf
10. To use an exaggerated example to make the point, if a low-resilience lawyer is criticized on a performance review, he might think to himself, "Wow, this is a terrible blow to my reputation. No one will give me any more work. I'll have to leave the firm. No other firm will hire me. Oh my god, I'll be unemployed. I don't have any other skill. I'll end up homeless..." By contrast, a high-resilience person might have a more "optimistic" set of thoughts: "Oh well. That criticism might have been warranted. It might be useful for me to hear what the critic's point is. Maybe I can learn some useful tips to improve my performance. Anyway, I've got a lot of other assignments that have gone well, so this one negative piece of feedback should be seen in perspective. And, I've been criticized before, and I recall that it hurts at the time but even two weeks later, it's just a distant memory. This too will pass." The latter thinking pattern has been shown to be found in naturally highly resilient people; those who adopt such a thinking pattern actually become more resilient.
11. Susan Raridon Lambreth, *The Practice Group Leader's Handbook for Success*, 2005. https://lawvision.com/client-resources/books/the-practice-group-leaders-handbook-for-success

Chapter 3:
Rethinking what your practice group is and might become

By Michael Roster, former general counsel of Stanford University and former managing partner of Morrison & Foerster's Los Angeles office

You've probably heard the old story about two buggy-whip makers. The first was very successful at making buggy whips, saw no need to change, and eventually went out of business once there wasn't much need for buggy whips. The second buggy-whip maker also was very successful but saw her business as making components for all modes of transportation. As a result, her business evolved into what became a major auto parts supplier.

Kodak invented digital photography but saw its primary business as manufacturing film and chemicals, considered Fuji Film to be its primary competitor, and therefore saw little if any need to market the digital photography that it had invented. It was on the cutting edge of innovation but then didn't bother to stake out its role until it was too late.

So how do you define the work of your practice group? If your practice group is highly successful, by all means keep doing what you're doing. But on the side, be sure you're also thinking about what your lines of business might be five and ten years from now, especially as we see the accounting and consulting firms expanding into the traditional work of law firms, combined with the emergence of multi-disciplinary practices (MDPs).

Over time, if you and your colleagues are good at it, you might find you are no longer just a labor practice group in a law firm, but a group of professionals that do all or nearly all of a client's HR and labor work, sometimes on an outsourced basis from your offices, and sometimes with your people located directly at a client's place of business. Similar transformations can take place with practice groups that do mergers and acquisitions, SEC filings, environmental compliance, real estate transactions, protection of intellectual property, and pretty much everything else now done at law firms.

Some law firm examples

Less than a year after I became general counsel at Stanford University and Stanford Medical Center, we outsourced more than 80 percent of our legal functions to a small group of law firms. The firms were awarded entire portfolios (HR, IP, tax, etc.), were paid monthly at largely fixed prices for each portfolio, were given offices on our premises if and when they wanted to function on-site, worked directly with internal clients without separate oversight from the remaining in-house lawyers, and as a result largely provided a turnkey service to our various operating units.

It turns out the law firm practice group handling much of our medical center's work had on its staff a former senior partner from one of the major accounting firms. And this wasn't someone who was semi-retired. Rather, he was in the prime of his career, had been a leading partner in the accounting firm's healthcare practice, and was now providing his skills and expertise to the lawyers at his law firm. Among other things, he monitored the profitability of the practice group's clients and thus was especially helpful in managing the fixed-price portfolios the firm had from Stanford.

A year later, we started doing some major corporate transactions at the medical center, leading eventually to several large reorganizations and mergers. This non-lawyer who was part of the firm's healthcare practice took on the role of helping us to manage these transactions. He developed project management plans, prepared pro forma spreadsheets for all of the participants (not just us) for both before and after the transactions, and even presided over many of the business meetings. Often, he told the lawyers from his firm they didn't even need to attend the meetings, especially when there were few if any legal issues to be discussed. Rather, he could monitor the discussions and identify what documents needed to be drafted and what other legal input might be needed. Our internal clients were delighted with the efficiency and expertise being brought to these matters, and the firm's lawyers could focus their time on real legal work, versus sitting around in meetings where few if any legal issues actually were involved.

This same law firm also had Stanford's benefits portfolio, including ERISA compliance, and had on its staff professionals who could handle the actuary and other issues that arose as part of our and other clients' benefits plans.

A different law firm had been awarded Stanford's environmental portfolio, and that practice group included not just paralegals but also other non-lawyer professionals who could address the types of issues that arise, such as air quality compliance, disposal of chemical and medical waste, and the like. Both law firms, without calling it as such, were developing MDPs, and very successfully so.

A non-law firm example

I was in London several years ago and had lunch with Richard Susskind, author of *The End of Lawyers?*.[1] That evening, I had dinner with a long-time friend and his wife. He owns and is CEO of a major food processor in Europe. I told him about my lunch with Susskind and also about the Association of Corporate Counsel's "Value Challenge"[2] and asked what his company was doing about its own legal costs.

"Oh, lawyers," he replied. *"We don't use them anymore."* He then told me about a UK company that provides a comprehensive service at a fixed price for HR and health and safety, the two areas that used to account for 95 percent or more of his legal costs. This entity largely doesn't advise his managers but instead performs the functions directly. That is, they write his company's employment and health and safety manuals; they update the manuals as they see trends among their many other clients and their interactions with regulators; they train his senior people as well as the workforce; and they regularly audit for compliance.

And then my friend noted, almost in passing, *"Oh yeah, and if we get sued, which almost never happens anymore, they have some lawyers who handle it"*. This result is very similar to what we achieved at Stanford with our major outsourcing/partnering years ago. When expertise is properly brought to bear, the number of disputes falls dramatically – at Stanford, after five years of the partnering/outsourcing, we had half the litigation compared to the prior decade, even while our legal costs had been reduced by 25 percent.

My friend in the UK loved the fact that what once was a major uncertainty in his annual budget – the costs of compliance and disputes – was now a fixed line item. It also was a huge benefit that the few disputes that now arose internally or with his regulators were quickly resolved and that he and his management team could focus instead on running the company.

If you think about it, what this MDP is doing for my friend and numerous companies like his is what law firms and in-house corporate counsel also largely do – we are monitoring for trends and deploying our expertise. But the MDP is able to directly solve problems, something law firm lawyers typically don't do.

Put more starkly, a practice group functioning as an MDP has the authority and expertise to be proactive, not simply reactive.

Platforms

In my opinion, the accounting firms will face major and possibly insurmountable challenges as platforms for MDP services. It may turn out they are too big, too rigid and, given their audit culture, too process-oriented rather than outcomes-oriented. In addition, eventually they will need to be split up still once again because of regulatory and company requirements that outside auditors be completely independent of any consulting and other business arrangements.

Law firms and their practice groups also will be challenged as efficient platforms for MDP services. Lawyers aren't typically trained to be business managers, especially over functions that aren't strictly lawyer-based. Our training is to identify issues (the "what if" part of what we do) but only a small set of really good lawyers are also good at the other half of the equation, which is "so what". That is, lawyers who have the expertise and confidence to decide what really matters for the client, what can be treated as a business risk instead, and to advise what a client actually should do. The megafirms will be especially challenged given their high overhead and income expectations versus the more granular pricing that is needed for MDPs to be competitive.

Much if not most of an MDP's work will be performed by highly skilled professionals who aren't lawyers, with the risk that eventually they will see no benefit in being housed in the large law firms that impose procedures that undermine efficiency and have overhead that undercuts competitive pricing.

One way for law firms to become more successful platforms for MDP services will be to give practice groups much greater autonomy in determining how best to staff themselves and price their services. Many practice groups would likely find they could actually increase profitability by reducing hourly rates, something that is anathema to most law firm chairs. Profitability would turn instead on a practice group increasing efficiency, as well as the number of clients served. In most cases, this would also mean pricing services at a fixed price and not by the hour. Rather, hours would be used, if at all, solely as a way to monitor internal costs of production and where the goal would be to continually reduce the cost of the hours as well as the number of hours needed to accomplish a specific task. A related goal would be for the practice group to be financially rewarded by clients for outcomes versus the lawyers' hourly costs of production.

Over time, there will likely be different concepts about time-to-partnership, the appropriate ratio of partners to non-partner staff, and the like. What works well and even is essential for one practice group may not work at all well for others.

The idea that a law firm should be run top-down by a dominant CEO also works against all of this. Rather, a law firm should see itself more like a hotel that provides space and basic services to its residents and otherwise stays out of their way.

Another analogy is to a university or medical center. Yes, we at Stanford or Amherst or Cleveland Medical Clinic all have a brand, and we watch for any departments that might not be maintaining the expected quality. But otherwise, each academic or medical department is fairly autonomous. That is, what an English department pays a professor is quite different from what is paid to a dermatologist or a heart transplant surgeon. And by the way, although the dermatologist's billing rate may be far less than the heart transplant surgeon's billing rate, the department of dermatology is often far more profitable than the surgery department. High billing rates do not necessarily equate with high profitability.

Another eventual approach will be to transition some MDPs to be separate subsidiaries or affiliates of the parent law firm. The risk here is the "heads I win, tails you lose" syndrome. If the subsidiary is losing money or barely breaking even after the parent law firm is reimbursed for support services and given a share of profits, the subsidiary's workers likely will stay. On the other hand, if the subsidiary is highly successful, its leaders and workers eventually will want to be spun off or will leave on their own. The issue is made even more complicated since a lot of the target market will be clients of other law firms who may be unwilling to refer clients to affiliates of competing law firms.

At least some MDPs may eventually decide that it is best for them to be wholly independent and where their officers and employees own and control the entity. These entities will likely be devoted to specific substantive areas and, as a result, everyone in the entity will have a common bond of expertise. There also will be much wider career opportunities throughout the organization. For example, a sales manager could someday be CEO, something usually not possible at a law firm. Likewise, the technology staff will no longer be part of a remote support unit that is stretched thin and often doesn't even understand what individual practice groups do. Rather, technology staff will be fully integrated with the business of the MDP and will often see major ways to improve efficiency and client satisfaction. Technology staff members might even be placed on site with various clients to integrate what the MDP is doing for those clients, including where the services are being offered on a totally outsourced basis.

Conflicts

Layered on top of all of this will be the problem of conflicts. The efficient provider of multi-disciplinary services will serve hundreds of entities in the same lines of business. Those entities may have similar issues but also periodically may sue one another, as well as do deals with one another.

As a general counsel, I never had a problem with a law firm or practice group representing my competitors in compliance and similar matters. I knew from my own days as a law firm partner that these firms and practice groups would have greater expertise and reliability because they were handling hundreds of similar matters and clients. My senior management was fine with that as well. What my fellow executives and board members couldn't accept was that a law firm or practice group with which we had shared highly sensitive information might periodically be on the other side, suing us. And what many law firm leaders don't seem to realize is, this doesn't turn simply on bar association rules of ethics. It's the appearance of it that impacts a company's senior managers.

I know many law firms seek blanket conflicts waivers. Most of us general counsel won't give such waivers but rather need to consider the issues case by case. I always bent over backwards to let my law firms and practice groups represent other entities. But as I said, it isn't solely a question of the rules of ethics, it's also how this comes across to my senior managers. If I tell my managers that they can share highly sensitive information with our outside lawyers and their law firms because the lawyers and their firms are truly devoted to the company, imagine how I come across if, a few months later, those same lawyers and firms are on the other side against us. And no, my telling my senior management that the firm (supposedly) has an ethical wall in place doesn't satisfy their concerns. For the law firm to properly maintain standards and deploy its expertise, its lawyers need to share information. So even if they don't name my company in their practice group meetings, they actually are sharing information about my company.

Privilege

Legal privilege will still be important and will be a problem for MDPs. It's why law firms that are devoted primarily or solely to litigation may have a strong advantage. But to be competitive, they will need to learn how to quickly and efficiently match up with MDPs that have expertise in specific substantive areas. This will allow the litigators to draw upon the MDP's expertise while developing and deploying successful advocacy strategies and still maintain privilege.

Possible transition

There are many ways for law firm practice groups to transition from their current methods to what I have suggested is likely to emerge for MDPs.

One way might be to informally divide the work of a given practice group between work that is best provided by a diverse group of professionals, not solely lawyers, versus work that is best provided via a more traditional law firm model. For example, a law firm's environmental practice might divide itself into an advisory and compliance group that is allowed to develop a different approach to that practice while other parts of the practice group continue to function in a more traditional way, especially when handling litigation and other forms of dispute resolution. Over time, the two groups would likely develop different approaches to pricing, including fixed prices; the addition by the MDPs of more non-lawyers, some of whom might be paralegals but many of whom might carry titles such as "compliance specialist", "advisory assistant" and the like; and over time the development of very different interactions with clients. As noted in my discussion about the European food company, the MDP entities might often provide their services on a total outsourcing basis for many corporate clients. Similar approaches might be tried for the labor, tax, corporate, and most other practice groups.

Parallel to those units would be groups that handle litigation or other types of disputes in a given substantive area, with the common feature being that privilege is very important for that group's practice.

Under this transition plan, practice group leaders and a law firm's senior managers could monitor how these parallel groups develop, but being in the position to someday spin off the MDPs into one or more separate entities. If there are such spinoffs, the original law firms might still offer support services, but with an understanding that management at the MDP would now be entirely separate so that privilege for the litigation group can be maintained, and likewise to avoid problems re conflicts.

During the period of transition, lawyers and paralegals would have time to decide which career paths make the most sense for them, and the practice groups likewise would learn what works well and what might need to be done differently.

If done right, MDPs will often be far more satisfying places to work, although lawyers may find they play significantly diminished roles, whether as outside or in-house counsel. As part of the transformation, the chief legal officer/general counsel inside various companies will often be replaced by a newly defined position of chief risk/compliance/solutions officer, who sometimes will be a lawyer, sometimes not.

I believe this transition is inevitable. The question for practice group leaders is whether they get ahead of the curve or find that these changes eventually are thrust upon them. The main takeaway: don't be that long-forgotten buggy-whip maker, and don't be Kodak.

References

1. Susskind, R. *The End of Lawyers? Rethinking the nature of legal services*, Oxford University Press, 2008.
2. www.acc.com/valuechallenge

Chapter 4:
Innovation in practice management

By Jonathan Fortnam, dean, Aston University Law School

Introduction

For years, innovation was genuinely discussed in law firm/client review meetings in the mutual (though unexpressed) understanding that neither side would be taken up on their proposals. It wasn't that innovation was feared or that both sides were necessarily wed to the status quo. It was just that everyone was too busy and when time literally equated to money, certainly *too busy* for the time and creativity that a serious commitment to innovation required. And no one really knew what innovation *looked* like. Lawyers are not often heralded for their powers of imagination and so it was perhaps unsurprising they conspired to "innovation lite" – reduced rates, capped fee arrangements, use of low-cost solution providers, and automation of usual processes.

As we embark upon a consideration of innovation in practice management, it helps to have some working descriptions upon which to base our thinking. They are not definitions. What falls within the scope of practice management is likely to differ according to the size, history, and culture of a firm. So, it is recognized that the descriptions may not be universally accepted as either complete or even accurate. Nevertheless, it will give us a common foundation for the thoughts that follow.

Practice management – a law firm perspective[1]

For some, or even most partners of a certain age, practice management is a distraction or even a disruption to the (literally) time honored, nuts and bolts activity of lawyers monetizing their time via the universally reviled (but probably unrivalled) concept of the "billable hour". The ability to convert time into money via the hourly charge out rate is not only the economic foundation of a law firm, but also the means by which lawyers measure their performance to keep their jobs and earn their bonuses. Little wonder when lawyers meet, the first (and somewhat unimaginative) question is "*Are you busy?*".

It follows that practice management embraces the people, processes, and technology (or perhaps, rather than "technology", infrastructure – it includes for example, facilities, a much more complex consideration post-COVID than ever before) that enable the efficient monetizing of lawyers' time. The people, processes, and infrastructure are many and varied – leadership (developing and delivering a strategy, inspiring and "walking the talk"), HR (the mission to attract, retain, and develop appropriate staff is a sizeable business in itself for most commercial firms), IT (covers everything from a new mouse to international cyber protection), facilities (everything from pens to premises), finance (money in and out), risk (how to avoid and if necessary, manage professional indemnity claims), marketing, development and training, and more besides.

With many overheads fixed for periods of 12 months or more at a time (rent, salaries, professional indemnity premiums, IT license fees, etc.) it is the role of the management team, headed by the managing partner, to drive income up (more of those billable hours please, or at least fewer unplanned write offs)[2] and to drive costs down, thereby maximizing the annual profit available to the partners (or in a more modern structure, the "investors" might be a more appropriate term). And when the finance department gets involved, it's about driving up charge out rates and, of course, the marketing team exists for the winning of new clients/mandates and increasing the amount of work done for a client ("cross selling").

Simple really… or maybe not exactly "simple", but in any event: WRONG.

Wrong because this description leads us to think of "practice management" as the exclusive preserve of the law firm itself and to be exclusively inward-facing. Yes, the partners in the firm own the firm, and are legally responsible for the firm (they meet a claim in the event of negligent advice). It's also the partners who first feel the effects of financial change in their firm[3] and therefore stand to benefit from a well-run firm. So, what is it to their clients how the firm is run?

Answer: a lot (or at least it should be).

Practice management – another perspective

For what goes on in the firm undoubtedly affects how its services and therefore its people are encountered in the outside world. We instinctively know this to be true and our instinct resonates with two concepts that we will briefly look at next. They are the stakeholder theory of business and the importance of alignment of interests.

First, the Stakeholder Theory was developed by R. Edward Freeman[4] in 1984 and could be described as a view of capitalism that stresses the interconnected relationships between a business and its customers, suppliers, employees, investors, communities, and others who have a stake in the organization. The theory argues that a firm should create value for all stakeholders, not just shareholders.[5] This broader view of business stands in contrast to a more conventional Shareholder Theory (from Milton Friedman, et al.), which in 1970 emphasized the importance of a financial return to investors of capital (i.e., shareholders) as the purpose of business and the measure of its success.

For law firms and law teams, stakeholders might be in the following categories:

- Employees (and remember in most law firms, approximately 40-50 percent of employees are not lawyers);
- Clients (and target clients);
- Suppliers (of facilities, IT, insurance, lending, etc.);
- Local communities (the people and economy in which a law firm and its stakeholders operate. Note: this is broad and can, for example, include the communities through which clients and staff journey to the law office); and
- Global communities (from politicians to polluters to professional and sector regulators across the globe, these are neighbors or perhaps "impactors", whether direct or indirect and who come in many shapes and sizes).[6]

If we focus on clients as stakeholders, a law firm's relationships with its clients are "mission critical". This is borne out by the thousands if not millions of pounds devoted to client relationship management and development, marketing, etc. Mission critical, and yet contaminated by a conflict of interests.

This is not a "conflict" in the legal professional ethics sense – rather, when we think of law firms primarily as *sellers* and clients primarily as buyers of services and, if the pricing is inherently uncertain and determined within an opaque system, a certain and profound tension exists. We will dig a little deeper into this conflict or tension before we consider whether it needs to be resolved either before or within innovative practice management.

Pricing – a client perspective

Businesses and their in-house legal teams are under pressure to reduce costs and get "more for less". More in this context is unlikely to be more lawyer output (enough already?!); rather it is more *value*. "Too long; didn't read" (tl;dr) illustrates the world in which business lawyers operate, so it's also a case of "less is more". Truth is (or at least might be) that clients want less output for less cost, but more value too.

At an operational level, in-house law teams are being asked to drive down costs, deliver identifiable benefits to their businesses, and to shed the "cost center" label. This pressure on costs has, in part, been mitigated by flow down into law firms resulting in discounted hourly rates, rewards for volume, "fixed"[7] and capped fee arrangements, which have in turn given rise to north- and off-shoring, on-demand contract services from lawyers without overheads, and so forth.

But this doesn't address the "less for less" dynamic opened up a paragraph or so ago; neither does it map into any law firm that uses chargeable/billable hours as a measure of success. So, if "less for less" (or "less" for anything) is here to stay, the existing/old model simply can't survive. There must be a management mindset innovation before there can be a technological innovation, and that has to involve a firm's clients.

Clients are, after all, free sources of feedback and otherwise expensive market research. Why wouldn't they be listened to? Why wouldn't a law firm want to resolve the conflict on pricing that lies at the heart of the mission-critical relationship? Answer: because the conflict has always been present and has never been tackled. So why indeed, and then, how?

Alignment – a new perspective

The theory of alignment has been around for some time and was famously captured in 1996 in "The 7-S Model".[8] The theory maintains that when Structure, Systems, Staff, Skills, Styles and Shared Values align with Strategy, the result is "*the creation of unique value*".[9] The creators of the theory state, with admirable simplicity:

> *"The underlying theory of the model is simple: an organization is effective to the extent it is well aligned; that is each S is consistent with and reinforces the other Ss. When an organization is poorly aligned, the organization will often exhibit problems and perform below its potential."*

If we apply the seven Ss into a professional services model, it is perhaps "Systems" that is most relevant for current purposes. Systems are described as:

> *"The formal processes and procedures used to manage the organization, including management and control systems*, performance measurement* and rewards systems*, planning, budgeting*, and resource allocation* systems, information systems and distribution systems."*

A traditional (or perhaps typical) law firm would expect to see billable hours in each of the * areas. And if we investigate "Staff", we see: "*How people are developed; … how their careers are managed*" and so more of those billable hours. Even "Skills" are not unaffected by the billable hours for they are "*The distinctive competencies that reside in the organization. Can be distinctive competencies of people, management practices…*".[10]

Clearly, billable hours run deep in a law firm. In addition, as they are part of the "*information that people receive and what they are measured upon and rewarded for [they] have a strong influence on what [staff] pay attention to and what they act on*".[11]

So, they run deep out of a law firm too, and yet they cause conflict with the law firm's principal stakeholder! Something must change to achieve alignment "*where strategy, goals, and meaningful purpose reinforce each other, [and] gives an organization a major advantage because it has a clearer sense of what to do at any given time*".[12]

The case for alignment is compelling but comes with a need to think clearly. In 2001, Cisco made what was then the biggest stock write-off in history ($2.5bn) because in the previous 18 months, it had incentivized the speed of its supply chain's responsiveness. As global demand for Cisco products stalled, its suppliers continued to supply – and very quickly. This misalignment of incentivized supply was later attributable to (i) a lack of visibility of others' actions in the supply chain, (ii) an imbalance of information, and (iii) a badly designed incentive scheme.[13] Alignment is nuanced and has to provide for different environments.

This is the place from which to consider innovation – but maybe we start in that consideration from a more realistic (if stereotypical) position.

Innovation: a different perspective

It is often said that law firm innovation is a difficult message to pitch to partners who are sharing handsome profits from well geared teams of "*insecure and overachieving lawyers*"[14] (amassing billable hours). Innovation is therefore often discussed under pressure from others, including clients. It can also be, initially at least, targeted at the automation of existing processes, for example, production of management information, including for clients. This innovation by automation is, according to Professor

Richard Susskind, "*A form of process improvement*" (emphasis added). He says, "*It involves the grafting of new technology onto old working practices*".[15]

The adoption of this automation has been substantial. The Law Tech sector has stepped up to the plate of opportunity and sold systems that enable clients to monitor a firm's time recording in real time, so they can see in real time who is working on their matters – Big Brother[16] would be proud. Whether this is progress or not has to be questioned. It might be an "improvement" that is designed to manage rather than cure a defective situation. For now, note the popular view shared at gatherings of in-house counsel: this technology addresses one aspect of the perceived opacity that besets law firms' time recording and therefore billing. However, and clearly, it does not cure the problem. Reports of law firms "gaming" the system in ways that result in new time recording narratives aren't what the client hoped for. By way of consolation, the technology results in a dataset upon which to base meaningful analysis and discussion at the next law firm panel review.

In September 2019, it was noted that most technological investment by law firms "*can generally be applied without dramatic shifts in mindset or in delivery of legal services*".[17]

For these reasons, the remainder of this chapter will focus on the need for and value of innovation in *lawyers' mindset* with particular reference to pricing of law firm services, rather than something that can be bought and installed. In so doing, we will face up to deeply embedded conflicts. For, in addition to the sell/buy conflict, clients also know that if they get the better lawyers on an assignment, they are likely to be pulled in many directions and possibly exhausted, at a time when they need focus and creativity; most in-house lawyers have worked in firms – and left to avoid "billable hours"; they will know and reject that culture (and be wary of claims that it has changed).

As a result, we have a situation in which:

- Clients have resorted to poring over timesheets (whether in person or via technology) in search of duplication or excess and consequent reductions in costs;
- Law firms feel they are being fleeced and certainly not trusted to do what was needed for a good job;
- Clients want (or at least said they want) "more for less"; and
- Law firms cannot countenance "less" for fear of compromised quality and possibly a professional indemnity risk.

It is time to be bold: if pricing is re-created, good things could follow.

Time for lunch

In-house lawyers sometimes get the chance to see different areas of their business and work with a variety of suppliers in ways that plan for and achieve sustainable and mutual benefits. If a particular approach works for those suppliers, might it also work for law firm suppliers?

Imagine one of several lunch suppliers to an office (say five: sandwiches, bakery produce, salads/fruit, chocolate, and drinks). A selection of sandwiches is made each morning and delivered in time for lunch. Demand is unpredictable because of competition (e.g., how could a salad compete with a hot pie on a cold day?) and so sometimes left over sandwiches are unsold; other times, stock sells quickly and potential further sales are lost. Sandwiches are best eaten when they are fresh and, without refrigerated storage on sight, the sales window is narrow. If someone is not around when the sandwiches arrive, sales are lost (potential customers go hungry and, tomorrow, may bring their own lunch). If either the cost of raw materials increases or the sandwich maker wants to increase profit, prices must increase. The change could result in lost revenue that is greater than that achieved by the price increase.

If the business persists in a seller/buyer mindset, these challenges will remain and may lead to a diminished customer experience (not only missed lunch, but also a reduction in the choice available as waste is sought to be eliminated). From the supplier's perspective, increased cost and reduced sales may lead to an existential crisis.

A collaborative mindset might however move into a different space: with the business purchasing a refrigerated storage unit on a "pay back" arrangement with the supplier, fresh sandwiches can be brought onto site each morning and deposited for sale over a period of time. Not only could sales increase, but variety can also be preserved and waste reduced. In due course, imagine a reduction in the number of suppliers so as to bring increased certainty into levels of supply (variety is less of a risk) and economies of scale into the cost of supply.

This type of arrangement, accompanied by a degree of financial disclosure to ensure sustainability for the supplier (failure is a joint problem), enables business and supplier to work together to achieve the mutual benefit of their stakeholders. You get the picture.

Arrangements of this nature (and more complex) are commonplace in businesses. What insight do they provide for law firms and their clients?

Redesign to align

Before we get into an example of innovation in this aspect of practice management, a few key thoughts:

- Responsibility for progress must be truly shared endeavor;
- Mutually desired outcomes must be carefully identified, aligned, and rewarded within the shared eco system; conflicting forces must be mitigated or removed; and
- Rewards must matter.[18]

A shared endeavor

Don't rely on just "getting along" with each other on the redesign team. A project of this magnitude requires communication of complex intellectual and emotional content. Consider joint sessions with an independent leadership coach in the expectation of uncovering purpose, a shared language ("Future, Engage, Deliver"[19] and "play to win rather than not to lose", etc.). This is especially important for difficult times when the team is tempted to give up and when traditions are being appropriately challenged.

There are usually three stakeholders who must share in the vision and its realization: business client, in-house legal, and external law firm. Time for the old adages ("We want to be an extension of the in-house team", etc.) to come to fruition. Listening and then discussing what the business client wants (and doesn't) can be revolutionary.

Mutually desired outcomes

It's time to own what you want from this redesign, and this can mean shedding a "We'll do whatever it takes to win your business" approach.

A degree of exclusivity in the supply of legal services could unlock a whole dimension of value. When the cost and uncertainty of "winning" the next job is removed from the law firm's activities, any diffidence in calling out ways to improve process and sharing innovative thinking can become normative. Repetition also paves the way for continuous improvement and even price reduction as people and processes become more efficient and effective in their working together.

Law firms need to respect the trust that is placed in them when that degree of exclusivity is bestowed. Clients will be concerned that law firms will no longer be "kept on their toes" if a competitive element is removed from the relationship. Truth is that, as with all relationships, trust develops in a more stable environment when no one expects perfection, and each is co-invested in each other's success. The shadow of the 1980s still looms large here: free markets, competition, and brace yourself for a cannibalistic supper of dog. Frankly, the time has come to move on.

If we are moving on, what better topic for movement than pricing. There are choices, but first it is important that interests are owned and planned for. So plan ways in which innovative arrangements (e.g., truly fixed prices for all assignments or phases of assignments) can be reviewed. Agreed minimum/maximum levels of profit for the law firm demonstrated through a form of open book accounting (I can hear the sharp intakes of breath). Mutual success benefits both parts (not sides) of a collaboration; success will be richer when it is co-owned and co-created. If the law firm makes less than the target profit, what changes can be made to make up the gap? If more, how can the benefits be shared (training, etc.)?

In fact, measuring profit has the potential to blow billable hours out of the water. It's what law firms actually want: billable hours are just one of the components of profitability and attract the spotlight as the first element in the journey towards being a profitable business. Fixed prices reward efficiency and insight, which means a business gets the answer in (say) five days not five weeks, or five hours not five days. Measuring profit means there is a meaningful incentive on the law firm to invest in efficiency. Increased efficiency preserves profit when its prices are either maintained or even reduced.

This mindset shift is significant and challenges many law firms' systems and understanding of success. Internal systems must be realigned to value a team that is looking to do less (*what?!*) to make more profit for the firm. Measuring profit is a step forward; it's not without its complexity – under recording of time is an obvious temptation. There is of course a sense in which the billable hour has always under-rewarded the most insightful and efficient. The call is to look at internal metrics and jettison the suspicion that, given the chance, motivated, high performing, and frankly, brilliant people will turn into work-shy wasters if someone somewhere isn't monitoring their time recording.[20]

Measuring success needs to be authentic and simple. KPIs risk driving superficial behaviors that focus on the service provider rather than the service user; systems thinking reverses the harm with a focus on a user's experience from start to end.[21] Think instead about user *satisfaction* – isn't that the sign of an arrangement that's working? It needs to be measured and it's likely the business has a trusted measure for measuring its own customers' satisfaction. The Net Promoter Score[22] could be used to measure responses to a question (just one – less is more!) that asks whether a user would recommend the law team (law firm and in-house team combined) to another. Reasons for answers can follow. Isn't this more appropriate than measuring the average time it takes to return a call?

Rewards must matter

Having mutually beneficial goals can help drive the team on when the going gets tough. Such goals have to operate at different levels in the combined team for them to work. So, how about agreeing that the in-house team will agree to provide references for the law firm to be used in pitches for new clients? Or the directories? At the individual level, might each play a part in the others' performance appraisal that informs promotion and pay for their people?

A final perspective

All very well to write about these things; all good in theory, but somewhat detached from reality. It's an obvious response. It's easy to be dismissive and instead to invest thousands on innovation that, frankly, misses the point or is doomed to miss the opportunities for profound and positive change and preserves the status quo.

But remember, the current situation is flawed, and this should not be a surprise. For years, innovation has been genuinely discussed in law firm/client review meetings. If these meetings can be re-imagined, and regarded other than as a distraction from the real work of getting the job done, they might not be so unpleasant ("excruciating", some have said) and become a time of creative problem solving that any serious commitment to innovation (and frankly to clients) requires.

As we emerge from the changes forced on us and our people by the COVID-19 pandemic, our sense that the old ways can't serve us well any longer is perhaps more acute than ever. With so many agile workers, we can't monitor what they are doing without systems that would be the envy of GCHQ. The way is open for significant and beneficial innovation that starts with addressing some of the realities. It's a no brainer, isn't it?

References

1. Somewhat stereotypical perhaps, but helpful for illustration.
2. Billable, but not billed.
3. First to feel the consequences of a drop in revenue when many of the overheads are fixed at least for a time and, likewise, first to enjoy the benefits of an increase in revenue.
4. Professor of business administration at the University of Virginia.
5. http://stakeholdertheory.org/about/ and many more academic articles.

6. At the time of writing, Russia is at war with Ukraine, oil prices (and therefore energy prices) are undergoing rapid increase, and driving up the rate of inflation in the UK.
7. Well sort of fixed, subject to assumptions, which means not fixed at all.
8. Organizational Alignment: The 7-S Model," Bradach, J. L., 1996, 9-497-045.
9. Bradach, J. L., *ibid.*
10. Bradach, J. L., *ibid.*
11. Bradach, J. L., *ibid.*
12. "The Aligned Organisation, the Lean Management Enterprise", Thierry Nautin, McKinsey & Company, 2014.
13. "Aligning incentives in Supply Chains", Narayanan, Raman et al, *HBR*, November 2004.
14. Laura Empson's insightful and powerful description of the prevailing mindset of successful lawyers and probably lawyers in general. See for example, "Are you an 'insecure overachiever'?": www.bbc.com/worklife/article/20180924-are-you-an-insecure-overachiever.
15. *Online Courts and the Future of Justice*, Susskind, R. (2019), p34.
16. *Nineteen Eighty-Four* (also stylised as 1984) is a dystopian social science fiction novel and cautionary tale written by English writer George Orwell. Though Big Brother does not appear directly in the story, his presence permeates Oceania's bleak society. Ubiquitous posters displaying his photograph feature the slogan "Big Brother is watching you"; hidden devices in every room enable his Thought Police to monitor the activities of all citizens.
17. Business Direction, Marcus Graham of Smith & Williamson (September 2020).
18. Nautin points out that "crafting the message [of alignment] requires care. Corporate metrics such as shareholder value may excite the CEO, but these tend not to excite employees. Instead, as with vision, the transformation message must appeal to… the individuals themselves, their teams, their customers, the organisation and society."
19. See Radcliffe, S., *Leadership, Plain and Simple*, FT Publishing (2012).
20. In fact, firms should be recording lawyers' time to protect from the manifestation of the insecure over achiever with the fear of missing out. For a starter, consider Sir Richard Branson's 2014 position on dispensing with annual holiday allowances and the risks of presenteeism: www.ft.com/content/1f3fa174-448e-11e4-bce8-00144feabdc0
21. Seddon, J. (2019), *Beyond Command and Control.*
22. www.netpromoter.com/net-promoter-score/

Chapter 5:
The increasing presence of non-lawyers in practice groups

By Neil Lloyd, managing director, FBC Manby Bowdler

The UK's justice system is widely regarded as one of the best and most independent in the world. For more than a thousand years it has changed and evolved – often at the whim of kings and men of power in the early days at least – but even in the 21st century, its evolution has continued to ensure our modern legal system remains fair and just for all.

One of the biggest developments in recent years has been the introduction of Alternative Business Structures (ABS). While many were skeptical in the beginning about the prospect of bringing in non-lawyers to manage or have a financial stake in a legal firm, it has not been the descent into "Tesco Law" that some had predicted. Quite the opposite in fact.

The 2007 Legal Services Act – which included the new ABS type of legal entity – ushered in a new era of competition in the industry and with it a push for firms to see and conduct themselves as commercial businesses. For a profession that had been less than forthcoming in embracing the world of modern business, there was now a green light to bring in expertise from outside the legal sector – permission to step out of the shadows of tradition and embrace new and exciting ways of running a law firm.

To do this successfully, the legal sector has needed to look outside the industry for recruitment – something that remains counterintuitive for legal practices even now. But there is a growing shift in attitude towards the appointment of non-lawyers to key business roles within law firms, and if done with the needs of the business in mind, it can be very beneficial to the firm, its people, and its clients.

I say this with absolute conviction, as it's a model we have adopted at FBC Manby Bowdler. We believe that bringing in senior professionals with their own areas of expertise gives us a fresh perspective on our firm and its operations, and we benefit from new ideas, which enable growth.

As the managing director of FBC Manby Bowdler, many people assume I am a lawyer, but in fact my background is in sales and finance. What I bring to the boardroom is commercial acumen, and that is helping to make the firm more profitable and propelling it forwards as a business.

Driving digital transformation

I first joined the firm from RBS as sales director in 2015. With my skill set and entrepreneurial approach, I was soon asked to lead both HR and new technology. As part of this remit, I led on the firm's digital transformation process. As a long-established profession with an obvious and understandable need to be cautious and thorough, it is easy to eschew technological development in the legal field and rely on tried and tested methods.

But technology is constantly evolving, and we need to be flexible and open to new ideas as they come to market. It's true that you have to move with care, attention to detail, and base decisions on solid evidence before bringing innovation to the delivery of our services. But with the right digital tools, we can make everyday processes easier, more efficient, and less costly.

Speaking from an outsider's perspective, I can see that, generally speaking, the legal sector seems to be resistant to the possibilities that digital technology offers, such as making routine tasks more efficient and leaving fee-earning staff free to do what they enjoy most – working with clients – or making a practice more accessible and user-friendly for customers.

Digital transformation has been widely adopted by almost every other industry from retail to banking. Coming from the financial industry, where technology has been well and truly embraced (they even have a name for it – fintech), I have seen for myself the far-reaching benefits of digital transformation and the potential for it to improve the efficiency of daily operations at the firm and to keep us at the cutting edge of how legal services can and should be delivered.

Under my stewardship, we have successfully introduced a number of digital tools that have had a really positive impact on the firm. We've adopted Settify[1] for our family department to allow us to provide prospective clients with customized, helpful information about our services. Settify is embedded into the department's page on our website, and it gathers a comprehensive brief of a prospect's divorce or family case at the initial online enquiry stage, so that we can tailor our response to the client from the very first call.

In 2020 we installed Introhive[2] to enhance our CRM to help us deliver a high-touch customer experience. Introhive monitors our relationships within the firm, tracking who is talking to whom, how many emails they are sending, and the quality of those emails. As such, Introhive highlights where we have strong client relationships and where we can make improvements, but it also helps with client migration and highlighting opportunities to cross-sell our services.

We also implemented HighQ[3] for our corporate team. HighQ is a collaborative site that can be used by both clients and our team, and it's really useful for complex projects where everything can be in one place. With its ability to improve workflow and productivity, and secure collaboration, HighQ may be rolled out to other teams at the firm in the future should it continue to impress.

We've even introduced a live chat facility on our website during business hours Monday to Friday – a function that is now available on pretty much every big commercial website.

Whilst we don't specifically ask questions in our client feedback questionnaire about their experiences with our client-facing technology, we do believe it's played a big part in our being rated number one for service locally on Review Solicitors, across pretty much every work type.

Little was I to know that all these digital processes would quickly become essential to the successful operations of the business during COVID-19. Without them in place from the outset, we could have had a very difficult time adapting to working remotely with our clients and with each other.

Developing a people-first culture

I took over the reins as managing director for FBC Manby Bowdler just days after the UK was placed into lockdown at the start of the COVID-19 crisis. Instantly, all the plans we had drawn up for the business during the handover period were overtaken by events. But then I thought to myself – why should leading in a crisis be any different to leading in normal times?

I had been working in the finance industry during the 2008 crash, so while I'd never experienced a world pandemic before, I had a pretty good idea of what resilience would be required to ride out the storm. And it started with our people.

I firmly believe that if you look after your team, they will look after your clients, which in turn leads to growth, and so on it goes. In my previous employment these principles had served me and my colleagues well, so improving employee engagement, wellbeing, and development was central to my HR plans for FBC Manby Bowdler.

At the end of 2019, before COVID-19 was even a "news in brief" in the UK, we appointed Sarah Bond-Williams to be our HR director. She was a senior HR professional in her own right, and I was keen to have someone on the board who would be focused on the impact and implications for staff during top level discussions. While the firm has a lot of solicitors who understand employment law, there was no substitute for having a qualified

HR specialist on board who knew how to engage employees, motivate, and develop them.

It's fair to say the first few months were tough for Sarah as, for some members of the team, the first contact they had with her was to discuss redundancies or changes of role. But after enduring the rough ride that was 2020 with us, 2021 was the year Sarah was finally able to find her feet with us properly and bring in some fresh perspective on our people and how we could improve their experience of working for FBC Manby Bowdler.

She has worked hard to build trust with our team of 200 and has brought in a number of initiatives that have been instrumental in improving engagement and galvanizing the team after a torrid 18 months. This started with a new leadership development program. We believe engagement starts with team leaders, yet in a staff survey, it was clear many employees were not getting regular one-to-ones with their line manager. As a result, they didn't feel heard, performance issues weren't addressed, and opportunities to discuss career progression were missed.

Sarah brought in a leadership development program to improve the core skills of team leaders to deliver more effective one-to-ones, and introduced a new booking system to ensure there were regular opportunities for engagement, performance management and evaluation, and monitoring staff motivation and wellbeing. Building emotional intelligence in dealing with people has been key to keeping a united team.

The provision of rewards and benefits can sometimes be a bit cold and contractual, particularly when they are provided without considering the bigger picture – what are they there for, who uses them, why are they a benefit? Our previous rewards scheme was only utilized by a small number of employees, so Sarah introduced a new rewards platform to offer a greater variety of benefits and discounts to incentivize and reward all staff. The new platform has additional features, such as online fitness classes, recipes, and mindfulness exercises, to support better physical and mental health outcomes for staff too.

Sarah was also ahead of the curve on creating more inclusive policies for the firm. Seventy percent of our workforce is female and Sarah recognized there were many important personal issues that were not being addressed by the firm, so we introduced new company policies covering adoption, IVF/fertility treatment, miscarriage, menopause, and domestic abuse to create a supportive and inclusive workplace for women and parents.

This kind of people-first approach requires the input of someone with wider industry knowledge of HR best practice, the employee relations landscape, and how to engage staff. But it also requires someone with that vision to be appointed to the board, where they have a platform to present ideas at the highest level, to support the overarching vision for the firm and to implement changes and initiatives quickly.

And what has been the benefit to the firm of bringing in Sarah to lead on our HR provision? We have increased staff engagement (as scored on the engagement multiplier index) to 79, we have considerably lowered recruitment costs because staff are not leaving, and we are promoting internally. We have over 80 percent of staff accessing the rewards platform regularly, saving them thousands of pounds at a time when inflation is squeezing household budgets. And we have created a more inclusive workplace, and as a result, we have identified vulnerable members of staff and given them the support they need.

Having that outside perspective on creating and delivering our people strategy has clearly paid dividends; it also reflects our broader thinking, of learning by looking outwards.

As a firm, we actively seek out alternate perspectives, many of which come through our membership of LawNet,[4] the collaborative network for SME law firms, with its agenda for leading edge thinking.

The network opens channels for our multidisciplinary team to share with other member firms, such as through LawNet's regular forum discussions, including those for leaders, marketers, and people managers. Members can drive the agenda by proposing discussion topics, and the network brings in experts to deliver valuable insights and stimulate debate between firms, tackling significant, heavyweight topics.

This exposes us, as participants, to new ideas, but also enables us to share our own innovation, and to validate decisions by listening to how others approached similar challenges and opportunities. Moreover, these sessions include both lawyers and specialists, bringing a further dimension for our multidisciplinary team.

The new business advantage

One of the mistakes that firms make when it comes to business development and attracting new clients is that it's a task delegated to already busy members of the team. More often than not, it's tacked onto a marketing role or given to partners or associates, as the more senior representatives of the firm. However, driving new business development requires a dedicated team and resources and it takes more than knowledge of our own legal practice to do it well.

In January 2021, we appointed Dawn Tuck to the position of head of new business. Dawn has a background in banking and finance stretching over three decades and she was brought in to focus on new business generation as well as to work with our existing clients to review their current legal arrangements.

Dawn is a chartered banker member with a diploma in credit. Like me, she doesn't have a legal background, but what she does have is years of experience in managing customer relationships, and that's the skills gap we were looking to fill and why she was appointed.

At the time, Dawn's appointment seemed to attract a lot of interest and fascination from our peers, as we were putting people from outside of the industry in key roles at the firm. But it is already paying off.

Dawn has oversight of our entire new business and business development operations, supported by her own team and resources. Our client relationships are still managed at fee earner and partner level (where appropriate) as these are the important day-to-day contacts and the ones with responsibility for ensuring our customer's needs are met and exceeded. But Dawn now has visibility of these different relationships and is able to look at our clients holistically – not just through the lens of one area of expertise.

For example, a client who comes to us for assistance with an acquisition might also need our support with employee relations for a TUPE transfer. It's about spotting the cross-sale opportunities to increase the client's spend with us. And with a helicopter view, Dawn is able to offer those insights.

A trial we ran in the early days of Dawn's tenure showed that from 45 annual legal reviews we'd carried out, a further 115 other opportunities were identified to help clients either with their legal requirements or by referring them to other professions such as banks, IFAs, or tax experts.

Bringing something new to the boardroom table

The one thing that unites Sarah, Dawn, and myself is that we are all specialists in our fields and we each bring a new dynamic to the FBC Manby Bowdler boardroom. We are there because of our core skills set – financial acumen, driving sales, creating an engaging and healthy culture – and we use these to develop our firm in ways that no one had considered before.

Our operational board, established in April 2020 when I took over as managing director, embodies the value we place on senior staff with specialist skills. It includes myself, Sarah, our finance manager, our head of marketing, our head of client experience and the head of risk and compliance.

The operational board meets weekly and is a complete melting pot of ideas, strategy, and professional experience. The discussions from the operational board are then taken forward to the executive board, which I sit on alongside two of the equity partners. We believe this gives us the best of both worlds, and a competitive edge too.

There is a saying that insanity is doing the same thing over and over and expecting different results. In a legal practice where only lawyers influence the decision-making, where is the innovation going to come from? How will the firm grow and develop to better serve its clients? How will it run more efficiently? How can it enhance its culture to benefit its people?

To enable change, you need catalysts – people that look at your operations objectively and see the opportunities to make things better. Without that outsider's view, you may not even know that something could be improved. After all, you don't know what you don't know!

The legal industry is steeped in tradition and I understand why its stalwarts seek to protect it from less scrupulous outside forces who want to somehow cheapen or dilute legal practice or degrade the skills and expertise of its highly trained solicitors. But there is much to gain from the knowledge and experience of people from outside the industry, and I believe there is a real opportunity to modernize firms and keep the sector evolving – as it has done for a millennium already – to ensure it remains relevant, accessible, and profitable for many years to come.

As more law firms come around to this way of thinking, we'll soon see even more non-lawyers joining practice groups, and that can only be a good thing.

References

1. https://settify.com
2. https://www.introhive.com
3. https://legal.thomsonreuters.com/en/products/highq
4. https://www.lawnet.co.uk/

Chapter 6:
Leading the practice group to sustainable profitability

By Norman K. Clark, managing principal, Walker Clark LLC

Practice group financial management – the law firm's transmission

Disappointing financial results in a law firm frequently – arguably, almost always – can be traced to problems in practice group performance. This phenomenon arises regardless of whether the firm has a formally organized, well-structured practice group or merely an informal, sometimes ad hoc, collection of expertise and service delivery capabilities. Conversely, the global COVID-19 pandemic has stressed the importance of the financial effectiveness of a law firm's practice group or specialty area. This was a time when many law firms faced the twin challenges of managing an uncertain and usually dwindling cash flow and scrambling to adjust their operations and service delivery infrastructure to new models. Across a wide diversity of firm sizes, practice specialties, and locations, two common characteristics of the firms that managed these challenges the most effectively stand out.

First, the relatively successful law firms, during the early months of the pandemic, had business plans for their major practice groups or practice specialties. Some of these were formal, standalone business plans for the practice; others were designated subsections of the business plan for the entire firm. The depth and detail of these business plans varied widely, from what could fairly be called sketchy to very detailed. However, it is no exaggeration to conclude that, on the whole, the law firms that had practice group business plans, even weak ones, managed the early days of the pandemic-related disruption better than those that had no plans at all.

The second characteristic enhances the first. The relatively successful firms also included some aspect of contingency planning in their business plans, especially at the practice level, where the impacts of a disruption would be more likely to have a greater impact than firmwide. Informed by at least a rudimentary form of risk analysis, these firms had already asked the question, *What if...?* Their answers usually needed refinement and adaptation to the actual nature and consequences of the problem, but at least these firms had a starting point to execute an effective, well-informed, well-considered set of responses. *Who could ever have expected…?* is not a useful response to any crisis.[1]

In all but the smallest law firms, therefore, the practice group is the "transmission" that converts aspirations into financial results. Business planning and financial management therefore are not just "business school exercises" or "nice to haves". Instead, they constitute a strong linchpin that communicates and connects the firm's business and strategic objectives to the people who must achieve them.

Four essential elements of effective financial leadership of a practice group

Each law firm and practice group is different, almost unique, in terms of their mission, the technical nature of the expertise that they deliver, the needs and expectations of the clients that make up their client base, their professional values and workplace culture, and the competitive forces in the legal services markets in which they operate. Cutting across this diversity are at least four areas of knowledge and practical skills that successful practice group leaders consistently demonstrate with respect to the financial management of their groups. The relative importance of each of these elements varies from law firm to law firm, and sometimes even among practice groups within the same firm, depending on the factors that influence financial success. They are as follows.

An in-depth, well-informed understanding of the specific factors that influence the sustainable profitability of the practice group

This requires two frequently overlooked pieces of business wisdom. First, as mentioned above, this understanding of sustainable profitability must include the possibility – and in all but practice-defined boutique law firms, the probability – that the factors that drive profitability in one practice, or even within a client industry sector, could vary significantly among practice groups. Second, it requires a willingness to accept the facts that define a practice group's financial importance, rather than deny them or try to explain away the financial reports and their implications.

A well-informed understanding of the current and future needs and expectations of the client base of the practice group

This includes an intense focus of the most important clients, who typically comprise only about 20 percent of the total number of clients served by the group but which collectively produce roughly 80 percent of the fees. Although every client, however small, deserves high-quality service that is professionally competent in every way, many law firms pay too much attention to the small clients and sometimes not enough to the ones that, as a group, produce most of the revenue.

Realistic, comprehensive business planning

Successful business planning for practice groups involves more than just good-faith projections. It also guides the actions of the members of the group in areas that many law firms do not consider, such as marketing and business development, client relations, risk management and business continuity, business and professional skills development, and the quality and continuous improvement of the processes by which the group delivers services to their clients.

Relentless continuing attention to quality

The most expensive failures, both financially and in terms of damage to a law firm's reputation, almost always can be traced to defective or unproductive operational systems and processes in a practice group. Yet, most law firm practice group leaders have a vague notion, at best, of what *quality* means in the delivery of legal services, and few of them address it in their business plans.

This chapter explores each of these essential elements of effective financial planning and management in law firm practice groups. Each of the four discussions offers practical suggestions, some of which are frequently overlooked or dismissed, and each can significantly improve and sustain better financial performance.

What makes your practice group profitable?

The honest answer for far too many lawyers is a shrug or a guess. A profitable practice group can "carry" practices in a law firm that are less profitable, but often this profitability cannot be sustained. The objective should be to maximize and sustain the optimal levels of profitability in every practice group. No law firm today can afford to have a practice group that loses money. The greater challenge, however, is not only to be profitable today but to be able to sustain a practice group's profitability into the future, uncertain as it might be due to changing economic conditions, the disruptions caused by *force majeure* events and conditions, and clients' rapidly changing needs and expectations for legal services. Whatever you do for your clients today probably will not be enough tomorrow, and, for some clients, whatever you charge them today for your services probably will be too much tomorrow.

The drivers of sustainable profitability[2] in practice groups are the same classic factors that lawyers have always had to manage, but some of the ones that previously were most influential for most law firm practices, such as price, have become less important in recent years due to increased client sophistication and its accompanying increased price sensitivity, even in practice areas that previously had been assumed to be relatively price insensitive. In other words, the client would pay whatever the lawyer charged, usually without objection or negotiation. Others, such as productivity and leverage, have become increasingly important and probably will continue to do so, due to opportunities that advanced information and communications technologies have presented to even the most traditional law firms.

A practice group business plan should therefore address each of the below six drivers of profitability as each one affects the group's specific practice. Moreover, the objectives for each of these six factors should be based on actual data from the firm's financial records, not estimates or educated guesses.

1. Pricing

Consider questions such as these:

- How do our fees (whether hourly rates, fixed fees, or some other fee structure) produce an average revenue per fee-earner hour that is greater than our average fully loaded operating cost per hour?[3]
- What trends in fee sensitivity should we expect among our most important clients? How can we overcome any such price resistance through a more convincing demonstration of the value of our services to those clients?
- How will we respond to client demands for deep discounts or success fees?

2. Productivity

Technology has already produced remarkable increases in lawyer productivity, as tasks that previously might have taken five hours, for example, now can be completed in half that time and with much better quality. Yet many firms still focus on the number of billable hours that lawyers record, particularly associates, as their primary measurement of productivity. This usually produces an analysis that greatly underestimates the opportunity to increase the value of the fee-producing work by increasing the volume that can be completed in the same period of time. This is one reason why, for most practice groups, fixed fees can be more profitable than the hourly rate.

For this reason, practice group business plans should consider and describe responses to issues such as:

- What will be our target to improve the average fee yield per hour worked (not per billable hour recorded)?
- Which of our current policies and practices interfere with productivity, and how will we remove or reduce these obstacles?
- What technological services and resources should we introduce into the work of the practice group in order to improve the productivity of fee earners and support staff? What will be their cost, both in terms of money and time? What return on that investment do we expect, and when do we expect it to appear?

3. Realization

One of the best ways to improve the profitability of a practice is to improve its realization rates. Even a modest improvement in a realization rate can produce disproportionately large improvements in profitability. Of the six classic drivers of practice group profitability, realization is probably the one that is becoming most responsive to market changes that affect long-term profitability. Disruptions often appear first as changes in the realization data.

There are three classic measurements of realization, and an inquiry into each one offers diagnostic insights and opportunities for even the smallest practice group.

- Recording realization – of all the fee-producing work (either under an hourly rate or a non-hourly fee structure) that we do, what percentage of it is actually recorded?
- Billing realization – of all the fee-producing work that is recorded, what percentage of it is actually invoiced to a client?
- Collection realization – of all the fees that are invoiced, what percentage is actually collected?

Even though recording realization is difficult to measure – how does one measure accurately something that does not happen?[4] – a bedrock component of a practice group's handling of realization should include a policy of universal timekeeping: every fee earner (and possibly support staff) records all work, whether fee-producing, administrative, or otherwise. Without universal timekeeping, the practice group denies itself important management data, as well as possibly revenue opportunities that are lost because billable work is never recorded and, as a result, can never be billed or paid.

Billing realization and collection realization not only point the way to increased revenue, but they also are important diagnostic indicators of problems in the way that the practice group works or manages relationships with clients. For example, if the billing realization rate is unsatisfactory – below 90 percent, for example – this often suggests problems that are relatively easy to correct, such as:

- Inadequate knowledge or skills of the fee earners assigned to do the work;
- Inadequate knowledge management systems, policies, or practices, resulting in unnecessary time and effort, particularly in drafting documents, memoranda, and pleadings;
- Unnecessarily time-consuming or inefficient internal processes in the delivery of a client service; or
- Inadequate or unclear communication within the practice group of the purpose, scope, or expectations concerning the task that results in a write-off or write-down of the fee.[5]

Unsatisfactory collection realization rates are usually indicators of problems relating to delivery to, or communications with, the clients. These typically include:

- Preventable errors in the billing process;
- Weaknesses in the firm's policies or practices concerning timely billing and collections;
- Client dissatisfaction with the results of the engagement;
- Vulnerabilities in the firm's credit risk assessment practices when accepting a new client; or
- Weak risk management practices to detect and respond promptly to changes in the client's financial position that might affect the ability to pay the firm's fees.[6]

One of the characteristics of practice groups that manage profitability effectively is that they pay close attention to realization and remain alert to significant variations in realization performance throughout the fiscal year.[7] The practice group business plan should reflect and remind lawyers in the group of the importance of realization by:

- Reinforcing the need for universal timekeeping in the practice group;
- Setting reasonable targets for billing realization and collection realization; and
- Outlining how the practice group will address known issues in their realization performance, as well as address significant variation from the realization performance targets during the fiscal year.

4. Cost management

Most law firms and practice groups manage operating costs reasonably well. However, there are essentially two measurements of effective cost management that are frequently overlooked in practice group business plans – fully loaded operating cost[8] and return on investment in marketing and business development. The latter measurement is especially important because many law firms and practice groups commit to marketing expenses, most notoriously attendance at professional conferences, with little scrutiny of the measurable business results that the firm can reasonably expect within the next 12 to 24 months.

During times of challenged profitability, it often is tempting to try to preserve profits by slashing costs. Targets for cost-cutting sometimes are obvious, such as reductions in facilities costs or staff reductions, and they sometimes can produce good sustainable results by eliminating waste in the firm's operations. However, poorly thought-out, impulsive cost management, even when it produces quick positive results, often make things worse in the longer term.[9]

A practice group's business plan should specifically address several questions that sometimes take additional thought:

- What is the fully loaded operating cost that the practice group will try to maintain during the fiscal year?
- What improvements in the practice group's fully loaded operating cost are possible, and how will the group try to achieve them?
- What will be the full cost, including the value of partners' time, in the group's marketing and business development efforts?

- What return on investment, measured in terms of potential fees, can the group reasonably expect to realize from their marketing and business development efforts in the next 12 to 18 months?[10]

5. Staff costs

Staff costs and leverage (see below) are closely related in the management of practice group profitability. As staff costs rightly continue to rise, in response to the need for more sophisticated support services, better leverage through more cost-effective delegation of work among the members of a practice group becomes the best opportunity to manage staff costs. However, some practice groups, because of their specialized practices in areas like intellectual property,[11] might discover that the most profitable way to reduce or constrain staff costs while maintaining high quality could be to delegate some of the work completely outside the firm by outsourcing it to expert external service providers who can deliver the same services at lower cost and with equal or better responsiveness, accuracy, and overall professional quality.[12]

A practice group business plan therefore should address staff costs specifically, including points such as:

- What, if any, opportunities exist to reduce staff costs without hurting the responsiveness or quality of the group's services to clients?
- What, if any, opportunities exist to outsource some core legal service functions to an external service provider?

6. Leverage

Most law firm practice groups tend to treat leverage somewhat superficially, as an academic concept, and therefore frequently fail to apply the analytical depth and intellectual rigor required to produce the significant results that are possible in the profitable delivery of legal services. The focus is almost exclusively on the weaker of the two forms available – staffng leverage – at the expense of the more important workflow leverage, which since the 1990s has become powered by the impact of technology on lawyer productivity.

Staffing leverage refers to the ratio of people, such as associates to partners or, in some firms, of all non-partner fee earners – e.g., associates, paralegals, legal assistants – to partners. *Workflow leverage* refers to the actual delegation of work, from partners to associates or from associates to non-lawyer fee earners.

Among practice groups in a law firm the actual leverage ratios often vary considerably, depending on the nature of the services that the group delivers. Therefore, assumptions about an ideal leverage – e.g., *a four-to-one ratio is the most profitable* – can be highly unreliable.[13]

At the other end of the spectrum, a high leverage ratio, whether of staffing or workflow, is not necessarily more profitable. Depending on the nature of the services delivered by a practice group, there is a point at which over-leverage – a six-to-one ratio is sometimes cited as a warning point[14] – can result in difficult challenges for partners to manage the quality of the work prepared by the people to whom they have delegated it, but for which they nonetheless stand accountable to the client. With technology increasing the productivity potential of associates almost every year (even a practice group with a relatively modest staffing leverage – four-to-one, for example), partners could experience a serious quality management challenge as the productivity potential for associates continues to increase. In short, the associates could flood them with work to review.

Law firm practice groups – especially the smaller ones, which usually are more vulnerable to the effects of information technology on their work – should consider addressing leverage-related points in their business plans, such as:

- What level of workflow leverage does the practice group try to manage?
- What measures will the group use to try to improve workflow leverage?
- What, if any, risks to quality could increased workflow leverage pose for the practice group, and how will they be managed?

Common forces with different effects on practice group performance

Three themes emerge from this overview of sustainable profitability of practice groups. Every law firm practice group on this planet will be affected by three forces that are sweeping across the legal services industry worldwide and in each national and local legal market. However, they will affect each practice group in a special, almost unique, way.

- The most obvious one is technology, with its potential for exponentially higher productivity and the potential benefits and challenges it poses for more profitable leverage of the work within – and in some instances, out of – the group.

- The continued, carefully selected use of outsourced services that previously were performed in-house can offer significant lasting benefits in terms of lower operating costs and better expertise and consistent quality. The quality-related advantages of outsourcing can also have the effect of reducing or eliminating errors which, if made in-house in the practice group, would have resulted in unbillable rework to fix the mistakes.[15]

These forces, and their impacts on the ability of practice groups to sustain better levels of profitability for their firms, should be new focal points for practice groups and key elements of their business plans.

Understanding the client base

Who are your best clients?

Most lawyers and law firm practice groups can quickly answer this question, but in many cases their answers are little more than partially informed guesses. The successful financial planning and management of a practice group requires a deep understanding of the group's client base – not only which clients are most important to the group's long-range success, but also why they are most important. These clients usually present the best business development opportunities, offering the best probable return on the firm's business development and client relations activities.

The 80-20 rule

There is a consistent 80-20 phenomenon that generally describes the distribution of fee production among clients of law firms. Roughly 80 percent of the fees come from only 20 percent of the clients. This ratio is approximate, of course, and it can vary significantly based on the nature of a law firm's practice.[16]

The 80-20 rule is not a best practice or immutable principle in the marketing of legal services. It is simply an observation of a prevailing phenomenon in most law firms, regardless of size or location. It is a diagnostic tool to identify specific opportunities to improve the fee performance of individual clients and, in some cases, to manage the risk of overdependence on one or two top clients.[17]

In addition to producing a disproportionate share of a practice group's fee revenue, these top clients are usually the most reliable sources of fees year after year, litigation clients often being an exception, and they are most likely to recommend the firm to others.

The clients in the lower 80 percent of the client base should not be ignored, however. The smallest clients usually do not offer a significant potential for increased fee performance. Nonetheless, the practice group should identify clients that are below the top clients, but who offer a realistic potential for more work in the future. The practice group's business development efforts should concentrate on these clients that have real potential to become part of the top group.

Where to target practice group marketing and business development efforts

The 80-20 rule is only a starting point for a deeper understanding of the practice group of a client base and to identify the best opportunities for marketing and business development. Practice groups should also focus on which of their clients, by industry sector or even by individual client, are currently the most profitable and which ones offer the greatest potential for future growth in fee revenue.

This analysis produces four basic strategic categories of clients:

1. High profitability and high growth potential.
2. High profitability and low growth potential.
3. Low profitability and low growth potential.
4. Low profitability and high growth potential.

The first two categories are the most important for the future financial performance of the practice group. The high profitability/high growth potential clients – sometimes called the stars – are where the partners in the practice group should concentrate their long-term investments of time, resources, and attention.

The second category, clients with high profitability and low growth potential, are also extremely important. Sometimes called cash cows, they are the clients who collectively make financial success possible for a practice group. They often are critically important to cash flow, and the profits they produce can be used to fund investment in the stars. The most important client relations strategy for this group of clients is relatively easy – pay whatever time and attention is necessary to keep the star clients happy. Service quality attributes such as responsiveness and availability of a partner are almost always decisive retention factors for these clients.[18]

The third category, with the low profitability/low growth potential clients – also known as the dogs – as a group lose money for most law firm practice groups. One exception is a practice group that provides high-volume, low-cost services to clients who produce substantial profits in other practice areas of the firm, such as a business immigration group that services major multinational clients with higher-value matters handled by other groups in the firm. Most practice groups, however, should avoid clients in this category unless there is a client retention benefit for the firm.

With respect to the fourth category – the low profitability/high growth potential clients, also known as question marks – the best approach is to look for ways to make the services delivered to these clients more profitable for the practice group. In many instances, the reason why a client with high growth potential is a question mark is that the practice group has overlooked or not yet implemented technological support that could lower costs and improve productivity. Sometimes, the relatively low profitability might be due to inefficiencies or ineffective quality control measures in the production of the service. Most quality-related problems can be resolved relatively quickly and economically, allowing today's question mark to become tomorrow's star.

Keeping up with change

The practice group, not the marketing department, is usually the best source of market intelligence about the changing needs and service expectations of a client, because the practice group usually is – at least, should be – closest to the client in terms of ongoing communications and knowledge of the client's business.[19] If a practice group conducts the type of financially-oriented analysis and planning described above, each lawyer in the group should be able to anticipate and respond to changes in the client's needs, expectations, and perceptions of value of the services that the firm delivers. Of course, this also requires frequent personalized communications, and not just reliance on end-of-matter client satisfaction surveys or mass mailed newsletters.

Realistic and comprehensive business planning

A practice group business plan should do more than just list some financial targets. It should also:

- Describe how the group plans to achieve those goals;
- Provide simple, reliable metrics by which the group can assess its progress and spot potential problems before they deteriorate into a crisis;
- Identify risks that could disrupt financial performance, and outline the preliminary responses that the group will take; and

- Clearly assign individual responsibilities to people in the group, in order to eliminate unnecessary duplication of effort and the risk of important actions inadvertently being overlooked.

The basic components of a practice group business plan

Like any business plan, the business plan for a law firm practice group is not only a planning document but also a communications tool. There is no universally optimal format or contents organization for a practice group business plan. In fact, it is often better if the practice group creates its own structure to a business plan than to try to insert content into a template that might be only partially relevant to the business realities in which the practice group operates.

Nonetheless, here is a suggested outline,[20] to be used as a starting point for further tailoring and refinement. Remember, however, that it is the quality of the content, not the format, that matters:

1. Summary of the financial projections.
2. Opportunities to improve profitability: specific goals, plans to achieve them, metrics, and assigned responsibilities for each of the following factors, as relevant to the practice group:
   a. Improved fee revenue;
   b. Improved fee-earner productivity;
   c. Improvement of realization rates;
   d. Improved cost management;
   e. Improved management of staff costs; and
   f. Improved leverage.
3. Foreseen obstacles and risks to achievement of improved profitability and how they will be managed.
4. Contingency plans to respond to major disruptions.
5. Opportunities among current clients.
6. Opportunities to win new clients.
7. New products and services (if any).
8. Initiatives to improve market visibility.
9. Initiatives to improve the communication of competitive advantages.
10. Staffing.

11. Facilities and equipment.
12. Summary of the key metrics that will be used to assess progress and to alert to possible problems.

These 12 points appear to require a long, complicated, and time-consuming effort. Indeed, depending on layout and formatting, a practice group business plan might require 30 or more pages. However, most law firm practice groups discover that their firms already have most, if not all, of the financial data necessary to create well-informed, realistic financial projections and, based on those, to estimate the return on investments of time and money in new initiatives. Moreover, the first time usually is the most challenging for lawyers and practice groups with no experience of this enhanced level of business planning. Most groups find that in the second and subsequent years, the experience of developing the first business plan, as well as the data that is compiled for it, provide a foundation that will make the process faster and more efficient.

Contingency planning – making plans you never want to implement

The COVID-19 pandemic and the disruptions in law firm operations that it caused alerted law firms to an important part of business planning, which a few law firms had practiced for years but which most had overlooked or had deferred as *we'll cross that bridge if we ever come it*. Today, however, contingency planning is a critical component of practice group business planning because it is practice groups that usually feel the impacts of unanticipated disruptions first and that usually are in the best position to develop practical responses.

The goals of contingency business planning are:

- To anticipate better the occurrence of a disruption in the legal services market;
- To be prepared to respond efficiently, ideally before the full effects of the crisis are felt; and
- To continue the operation of the practice group at the same or better levels of financial performance.

This third goal is not just wishful thinking. Many law firms throughout the world, of all sizes and in almost all practice specialties, reported that although fee revenues dropped sharply in the 2020 fiscal year, profits – such as those measured by average profits per equity partner – actually increased, due in part to much lower operating costs as offices closed and people worked from home.

Spotting and at least preliminarily assessing the risks of economic disruption requires closer and more comprehensive attention to economic forecasts and emerging business trends than many lawyers – who prefer simply to practice law rather than take up macroeconomics as hobby – traditionally have paid. Lawyers in practice groups, even in the largest firms, have a special advantage in such a risk analysis exercise. In addition to being able to learn about the macroeconomic risks and developments, they often have a front-row seat to observe the practical business impacts on their clients. Practice groups and their clients, therefore, can be a highly effective "distant early warning system" for any law firm.

What should a contingency business plan for a practice group contain? Above all, it should be an integrated part of the group's annual business plan, not a separate document, which can easily be filed away and forgotten. It should be a relatively simple document, with these features:

- It should focus on a range of possible *force majeure* events, not just a pandemic or normal business downturn.
- Most contingency plans for practice groups do not need to be more than two pages long for each contingency being addressed.
- Whenever possible, a practice group contingency plan should link to and implement a firm-wide contingency plan.
- The typical focal length of a practice group contingency plan is 12 to 24 months. Therefore, some contingency plans "roll forward" from one annual business plan to the next, being updated as necessary to reflect new assessments of the risk that is being addressed.
- Even if a contingency plan covers two years or more, it should be reviewed and updated as needed as part of the annual business planning process. This is important for two reasons: (1) it helps keep contingency planning in the context of, and relevant to, the financial performance of the practice group; and (2) if updating is set aside to be a separate event, it probably will be forgotten or done only in a cursory manner.
- The contingency plans should consider worst-case scenarios. This makes it easier to scale back the response if less drastic results occur. Moreover, as recent events have demonstrated, sometimes the worst cases are not as improbable as one would hope.

- Finally, in addition to their general contingency plans, some firms also develop contingency plans to continue services to their financially most important clients.

Relentless and continuing attention to quality

Quality in legal services is more than using spell-check or returning calls the same business day. It requires meeting the client's needs and expectations the first time and every time. The most expensive failures in the performance of a law firm can almost always be traced back to defective or unproductive operations and procedures at the practice group level. As W. Edward Deming said, *"A bad system will beat a good person every time"*.[21]

The best place for any law firm, regardless of size, to focus on quality management as a profitability tool is in the practice group. This is where the work gets done. This is where costly mistakes get made. This is where one can find the people who are best qualified to address the problems permanently – not efficiency experts or outside consultants, but the people who actually do the work. They know the work best, and with the proper concepts, tools, and methods, which anyone can learn, they are in the best position to improve it.

Quality management is perhaps the last remaining undeveloped area in practice group leadership in most of the legal services industry. Marketing slogans, artificial "team-building" seminars and exercises, and exhortations to the workers and staff seldom produce any lasting improvements. At best, a short time after these superficial events and experiences, most practice groups, like most units in other business organizations, slip back into old ways and resume making the same old mistakes.

Quality management is more than post hoc detection and fixing of mistakes. Instead, it focuses on identifying and understanding the causes for profit-sapping inefficiencies, errors, and unbillable rework. Instead of investing time to fix mistakes after they happen, lawyers and staff can prevent mistakes from happening in the first place.

Some aspects of quality management seem to fit comfortably into the professional cultures of most law firms. Quality management focuses on how the client defines quality – and, from that, value – in the services delivered by the law firm, rather than on a traditional, academic – and usually somewhat self-congratulatory – definition of quality by lawyers. Most law firms, due to the competitive need to focus on meeting the client's needs and the keen sense of personal responsibility that most lawyers feel toward their clients, embrace this easily. The concepts of fact-based analysis and frequent feedback driving permanent and continuous improvement also appeals to the intellectual discipline of most lawyers and business managers in law firms. Finally, and most importantly, there is the strong steady link of quality management to clear, measurable financial results.

Nonetheless, practice group leaders should be prepared for some other aspects of a "quality culture" that might be uncomfortable among their colleagues. For example, disappointing results or even failure are not something to dread, but instead are data that can point the way to a better solution. Instead of trying to hide mistakes, which is common in many law firm environments, people need to be encouraged by their leaders to report mistakes when they occur, because errors can often alert the group's leaders to previously unnoticed or subtle problems and from that can point the way to sustainable improvements.

This is why quality management has become one of the most important skills in the financial leadership and management of law firm practice groups. The most significant opportunities to improve the overall profitability of a law firm will usually be found in, and accomplished by, its practice groups. The concepts and methods of quality management thus have become essential tools for practice group leaders.[22]

Where the action is

The issues, trends, and discussion in this chapter point to the increased importance of the practice group, whether formally constituted or just an informal group of lawyers who collaborate on similar matters, to the financial performance of a law firm. Instead of being a tiresome academic exercise, business planning for practice groups allows group leaders and their colleagues to gain more accurate knowledge and deeper understanding of what it will take for their groups to succeed, with clear and direct consequences for the overall financial performance of their law firms. In short, it is in the practice groups in most law firms where the opportunities are and the action should be, in terms of sustainable profitability, strengthening of the client base, more effective responsiveness to crises and risks, and better profitability through quality management that is more than a slogan on the firm's website.

The practice group business plan, if prepared with good information, intellectual curiosity and discipline, and insight into the evolving and sometimes rapidly changing needs and expectations of the group's clients, can document how the group plans to achieve its goals and, more importantly, can serve as a practical guide to their achievement.

References

1. These conclusions are based on observations and confidential discussions with the managing partners and practice group heads of a sample of more than 40 clients of Walker Clark LLC, conducted between April and December 2020.
2. See, generally, Norman K. Clark and Lisa M. Walker Johnson, *Sustainable Profitability in a Disrupted Legal Market* (Globe Law and Business, Ltd, 2019).
3. Fully loaded operating cost is the total operating cost of the law firm for one year. In addition to basic costs such as facilities, equipment and supplies, it includes salaries and benefits for staff and lawyers who are not equity partners. Fully loaded operating costs do not include purchases and investments paid from the capital of the firm or financed externally. When used to ascertain the profitability of a fee arrangement with a client, the average fully loaded operating cost per fee-earner hour is a reasonably reliable indicator of the profitability that a practice group can expect from a matter. It is an especially powerful financial indicator for a practice group, because it can take into account the particular nature of the work and staffing required to deliver the engaged service to the client, and how that work might be different from that in another practice group in the same firm. See *Ibid.*, pp. 60-62 for a further discussion and example of how fully loaded operating cost per fee-earner hour can be calculated in a practice group.
4. Research conducted by Walker Clark LLC consultants, using anonymous interviews of law firm associates in several law firms since 2002, suggest that approximately ten percent of otherwise fee-producing work is not recorded. The two most frequent reasons ascribed are: *I forgot*; and *I assumed that the billing partner would write off that time had I recorded it, because the task took too long to complete*. Moreover, there is a very high correlation between I forgot and not recording the time the same day that the work was done.
5. Clark and Walker Johnson, *op. cit.*, p. 54.
6. *Ibid.*
7. Variation in the realization rates is more significant than the actual percentage. Variation is a natural phenomenon in the financial performance and productivity of a practice group – indeed, in any human activity. Some organizations overreact to relatively minor variations in performance, a tendency the author calls *chasing the numbers*. Significant variation, however, is usually a reliable indicator that something needs attention. If there is a significant decrease in a realization rate, that could be a sign of a hitherto undetected problem in the way that the work is being done. Conversely, a significant upward variation might indicate something that at least some members of the practice group are doing very well and that should be replicated. Variations in realization rates warrant attention, however, when either of the following conditions appear:
   - There is no apparent external explanation or one-time cause for the variation.

- The change in performance has continued for at least three consecutive months or for three months during a period of five consecutive months.
- Wide variations from month to month suggest that realization is out of control.

8. See note 2, *supra*.
9. Clark and Walker Johnson, *op. cit.* pp. 59-68. For example, some of the most common mistakes in cost-cutting at the practice group level include:
   - Cutting costs without first having calculated the practice group's fully loaded operating costs and the extent to which the proposed cost-cutting measures would have any significant positive effect;
   - Overinvestment in multiple offices, particularly those that are opened essentially as marketing outposts rather than working, fee-producing sites;
   - Not keeping up with advances in information technology;
   - Ignoring partner performance issues; and
   - Slashing costs without managing risks.
10. This is what distinguishes a plan from a guess or a well-intended wish.
11. See, e.g., Tushar Gupta and Gaurav Khandelwal, "Patent drafting, research, analysis," in Norman K. Clark, ed., *Outsourcing of Core Legal Service Functions: How to Capitalize on Opportunities for Law Firms* (Globe Law and Business, Ltd, 2021), pp. 17-42.
12. Outsourcing is not a cost-effective option for every practice group. When considering outsourcing of a core legal function, a practice group should first identify the specific processes or functions that cost the most to perform in-house and pose the highest risk of errors. For an example of this analysis, see Norman K. Clark and Fernando Moreno, "The business case for the outsourcing of core legal service functions," *Ibid.*, pp. 10-13.
13. For example, it is not unusual to find Latin American firms with overall staffng leverages of five-to-one or six-to-one. In fast-growing legal markets, like those in Latin America and Asia, most of the growth in law firm size takes place at associate level, while the number of partners tends to grow more slowly. In some instances, this disparity in growth reflects a need to manage the financial, administrative, and practice management transition from a firm's founding partners to the next generation. Clark and Walker Johnson, *op. cit.*, p. 79.
14. Walker Clark LLC consultants have observed that, in corporate and commercial practice groups for example, once the leverage (staffing or workflow) rises above six-to-one, and unless the group already has strong quality management procedures in place, there is a corresponding increase in errors in the work, resulting in unbillable rework to correct mistakes that could have been prevented if the supervising partner did not have to supervise such a large volume of work in addition to managing his or her own.
15. In some respects, the basic operating model of law firms is changing from a "factory

model" in which substantially all the elements and components of a legal service are prepared and produced in-house for delivery to the clients, to a "shipyard" model by which the law firm "assembles" components, such as intellectual property research and analysis or high-volume document review, from external suppliers, to meet the exact specifications that the client requires. See, Norman Clark, "The Law Firm of the Future: from 'factory' to 'shipyard'," *Walker Clark World View* (15 February 2022) www.walkerclark.com/worldview-blog/431-the-successful-law-firm-of-the-future-2-shipyard.html.

16. While conducting analyses of the client bases of law firms and law firm practice groups over the past 20 years, Walker Clark LLC has observed and continues to observe this phenomenon, which was first identified and documented in the research conducted in the late 1990s by Jay Curry. See Jay Curry, *The Customer Marketing Method: How to Implement and Profit from Customer Relationship Management* (Free Press, 2000). The 80-20 rule should not be assumed to be a benchmark; it is merely descriptive of the research that Curry, Walker Clark LLC, and others have done. A law firm or practice group that specializes in high-volume, relatively low-margin legal services, such as trademarks administration or patent prosecution, can produce a distribution that is closer to 60-40, i.e., 60 percent of the fees coming from 40 percent of the clients. Firms that engage primarily in major complex litigation might, in a given fiscal year, have only two or three percent of the clients producing as much as 50 percent of the fees. However, for most commercial law firms, the 80-20 rule, plus or minus five percent on either side of those marks, usually prevails.
17. For example, if a law firm has a client that produces more than 20 percent of its fee revenue, it could be overly dependent on that single client, risking severe financial consequences if that client suddenly departs. This warning value, like the 80-20 rule, can be highly practice-specific.
18. The Walker Clark Strategic Business Development Survey consists of a database of more than 3,600 responses from decision makers and influencers in the major clients of law firms, compiled since 2002. It asks respondents to rate the importance (i.e., decisive, important, secondary, or unimportant) of a set of 20 factors in the client's decision to engage a law firm or to instruct it for further matters. Of these 20 factors, responsiveness and availability of a partner rank first and second, with responsiveness significantly ahead of availability and the other indicators. Interestingly, low price is almost always rated as secondary, and ranks 16th out of 20. In the past ten years, *responsiveness* has increased its lead over the other 19 factors.
19. *Understands my business* ranks fourth out of the 20 factors in the Walker Clark Business Development Survey.
20. This outline is developed from practice group business plans that have been

produced by client law firms of Walker Clark LLC. It must be tailored, however, to the special characteristics of each practice group. Depending on how a law firm funds and manages activities such as firm-wide marketing, as distinguished from practice group marketing, facilities maintenance, capital investments in facilities, and staffing, some of these 12 points might be unnecessary to address except to the extent that they might influence the analysis of opportunities to improve profitability.

21. W. Edwards Deming's address at the Deming Four Day Seminar (Phoenix, Arizona, February 1993). For further information about quality management generally, visit The W. Edwards Deming Institute, https://deming.org.
22. Two examples from among the author's many experiences with quality management in practice groups demonstrate the high return from investing a small amount of fee-earner time, and an even smaller amount of money in process improvement.

    The first was a tax collections practice group that was responsible for filing tax recovery litigation on behalf of the tax authority against delinquent taxpayers. The work was high-volume, with relatively low profit margins, relatively unsophisticated, but heavily document-driven. Law firms handling these matters were required to commit to standards for average processing times. These standards had been challenging, and the practice group had done reasonably well in meeting them, but they believed that they could do better. A group of fee earners and staff in the practice group flow-charted and reviewed their documentary processes to identify and reduce the causes of errors and delay. In less than two months they were able to cut their processing time by more than 25 percent with no reductions in staff, largely by eliminating unnecessary duplications of effort, thereby creating additional work capacity that would produce "pure profit" from the new work they could accept. Their improved processing times enabled them to expand substantially their instructions by being able to commit with great confidence to much faster processing times than any of their competitors could meet.

    The other example is a finance litigation practice group that was on a panel of law firms for a major bank. As part of its management of the work by the panel firms, the bank conducted semi-annual audits of the bank's case files, to ensure that the matters were being conducted in compliance with the bank's standards. The practice group failed an audit and was in danger of losing a major client unless they addressed the problems detected by the audit. A group of lawyers and paralegals met for two days, analyzed the processes by which the bank's cases were handled, and identified the points at which errors (mostly missing or incomplete documentation of major events in the case) occurred. They developed specific measures, involving quality management measures such as more frequent review of the case files and case status reports, to address the causes of the defects found in the audit. At the next audit, several months later, the group received one of the highest scores ever achieved by any law firm on the panel. An important part of this example is that the team's work totaled under eight hours and produced quality management protocols for each of the four distinct processes that they improved, each protocol being under four pages long.

Chapter 7:
Developing a practice group pricing strategy

By Colin Jasper, principal, Positive Pricing

Introduction

No lever has a greater impact on the financial performance of a practice group than price. If a practice group has revenue of £1m per partner, a five percent improvement in pricing equates to additional profit of £50k per partner. A five percent improvement in pricing can be achieved through:

- Higher rates (e.g. £420 per hour rather than £400);
- Lower discounts (e.g. five percent rather than ten percent);
- Lower write-offs (e.g. ten percent rather than 15 percent);
- Having higher project prices (e.g. £21k rather than £20k); or
- A combination of one to two percent on several of these.

The only lever that has the same impact as price is utilization, which in turn is impacted by price. When the price is too high, utilization drops. An effective pricing strategy should keep valuable resources busy, while maximizing the financial return on these resources.

Given the impact of pricing on a practice group's success, it's essential that practice group leaders ensure an effective pricing strategy exists for the group. While the firm may have processes in place for setting rates and approving discounts/write-offs, the pricing strategy needs to go well beyond this to focus specifically on how the practice group will:

- Maximize the value created for clients; and
- Capture a fair share of that value for the firm.

As most law firms are quite diverse in the services they provide, it is generally inappropriate to develop a pricing strategy at the firm level. A litigation group's approach to pricing is likely to be very different to the approach taken by a real estate group. The key pricing challenges faced by each group will differ depending on the practice and the nature of the clients. And while each group needs to demonstrate value to their clients, the way this is achieved will vary significantly.

Ideally, the pricing strategy should be developed collaboratively with partners to ensure both broad input is obtained, and the resulting strategy is owned by those responsible for implementing it. The resulting document should be no more than two pages, so that it can be referred to easily and provide day-to-day guidance for those in the practice group.

This chapter explores what should be included in a pricing strategy and how to create one for your practice group, including:

- Targeting clients and services;
- Setting prices;
- Justifying why we should be chosen (even if we are more expensive than competitors); and
- Managing matters.

Targeting clients and services

A common refrain within the legal sector over the last decade has been concern regarding the market shift towards commoditization. The reality is that all products and services commoditize over time. Many lawyers believe that pricing power has shifted to clients. The truth is that both clients and firms have equal market power. Any price is an agreement between buyer and seller. If the client doesn't like the price, they can choose to buy elsewhere or not buy at all. If the law firm doesn't like the price, they are not compelled to provide the service. Having said that, price-sensitivity differs by client. It is difficult to have a financially successful practice if we are working for the wrong clients.

A simple exercise to identify the ideal target market is as follows. Ask partners to list the characteristics of price-sensitive clients. This may be to do with client size, industry sector, the way they purchase legal services, or even attitudinal characteristics of the buyer. Partners generally find this easy to brainstorm. Everyone has an example and a frustration to share. Then ask partners to list the characteristics of "less price-sensitive" clients. It should provide a contrast to the first list. The question then becomes how to attract more clients from the second list, so that we have the freedom to walk away from the price-sensitive clients.

Depending on the nature of the group, the exercise can be repeated for the range of services provided by the group. Are some services more/less price-sensitive than others and as such should we be aiming to alter our mix of services as we move forward? Input into this exercise can come from the group's financials. Which matters are more profitable than others? Which matters have lower write-offs?

An additional overlay that may also need to be considered is which clients/services offer the greatest growth opportunities. Ideally, we want to be focused on areas where we can expand with the market. For many partners the day-to-day reality is that clients complain about price and when work is lost they are told it was because the price was too high. Because of this, identifying the right target clients and services is an important first step in developing a pricing plan. It often provides partners with the confidence that they can achieve better financial outcomes if they are able to shift the focus of their practice.

Setting prices

Within law firms, prices are generally set in the following stages:

The first step is to determine appropriate charge-out rates for each fee-earner. While this is often thought of as a costing exercise (i.e. apply a 2.5-3.0 times multiple of salary), it is better considered as an optimization exercise. At what rate will we maximize revenue (utilization times price).

Many firms like fee-earners at the same level to be on the same charge-out rate. While this may be appropriate for junior levels, it becomes less appropriate the more senior staff become. If all partners are on the same rate it is achieved by pushing some partners to charge more than what their market justifies (resulting in an inability to sell sufficient hours) or by under-charging other partners (resulting in reduced profit to the firm).

Through the course of my consultancy work I have conducted pricing audits on a range of professional service firms. These audits are focused both on improving the firm's pricing capability and on identifying immediate opportunities to improve price. The most common opportunity for immediate gain is identifying partners whose rates are too low. They are easy to identify. They are the partners who were fully utilized last year and the year before – and are expected to be fully utilized again this year and next. Economics 101: if demand outstrips supply, increase the price. For one global firm, we identified a range of partners who sat in this category. We increased their rates considerably and they were all still fully utilized the following year. The only difference was that they generated over an additional £3m in revenue that year. All profit!

Which fee earners in your practice group should have a higher rate? These opportunities exist in many firms because pricing has historically focused on problem areas. Areas where we are finding it difficult to charge what we would like or areas where we are experiencing excessive write-offs. Generally, the easy opportunities exist where pricing has not been a problem. When the price sought is easily captured, perhaps it's because we are not asking enough. Similarly, many firms use client feedback on pricing as a key input into pricing strategy. This is a mistake. Most of the feedback received will be from the price-sensitive clients. More attention should be placed on the silent majority – the clients who accept the rates and willingly pay the bills when due. While it's appropriate to base pricing strategy on client behavior (are they collectively buying or not?), it's inappropriate to create a pricing strategy based on client feedback.

Many clients (particularly large clients) now expect discounts on standard rates. The reality is that realization (i.e. collected rate vs standard rate) has declined. Once clients have been offered a ten percent discount, they are not going back to a five percent discount. That said, realized rates continue to increase. This highlights that standard rates are increasing at a faster rate than discounts.

When setting matter prices (these may be estimates that are treated as caps), it is appropriate to consider not only hourly rates but also market prices (i.e. what are competitors likely to charge?) and the value of the matter to the client. In setting matter prices, I have seen great value in establishing a peer review process. The benefits include:

- Greater consistency – are we all charging the same for similar services?
- Increased confidence – if the client pushes back on the price (which they are entitled to do) I am more likely to have confidence in my pricing if a peer has reviewed.
- Addressing personal insecurities – one of the key issues preventing improved pricing performance for many professionals is their own self-confidence. These individuals consistently under-charge unless processes are in place to prevent it.

This section of the pricing strategy should cover:

- How standard rates are set, including which rates should be increased now;
- Which clients should be offered discounts (and which shouldn't) and the process for approving such discounts; and
- How matter prices are reviewed.

Justifying why we should be chosen, even if we are more expensive than competitors

It's very easy to fall into the trap of believing we need to compete on price, but for all but one firm (the cost leader), there is always going to be someone cheaper. Choosing to compete on price is choosing to behave like a commodity.

Ultimately, it's our role to justify why we should be chosen, even if we are more expensive. Fortunately, few clients choose a law firm based on price. Most clients will say that if they find a lawyer with the right expertise to assist them on a matter, who understands their issues and needs, who they like and trust to look after their interests, then they will use them – provided the price is fair and reasonable. To prove this point, you may wish to run the following exercise with your partners. Ask each of them to think about a client or a matter that they have won in the last three to six months. Ask them why they won the work. When I have run this exercise with groups of partners the most common responses are around:

- Expertise – including track record, past projects, and reputation; and
- Relationships – including prior work, knowledge of the client, and personal relationships.

Occasionally price is also mentioned. At the very least this exercise should remind partners that we don't have to compete on price. It should also point to the primary reasons we should be chosen, even if we are more expensive. This leads us down the path of building our reputation in targeted areas (to become a visible expert) or building relationships with targeted clients (to become a trusted advisor).

Having developed a clear plan on how we aim to compete, we should also help clients understand that the price is fair. Pricing is never about the absolute value. If you tell me this matter will cost £40,000, I don't know if that's a good price or not. The only way I have of assessing this price is to compare it to something. Presented in isolation, my most obvious means of assessing if the price is fair is to obtain a quote from a competitor. But we have other options for helping clients understand that the price is fair, including:

- Comparing the price to what's at stake – what's the impact of the work we are doing (i.e. the business case). When the stakes are high, competitors' prices become less relevant.
- Providing the client with options (i.e. different ways to engage us at different price points) – if you provide a single option to a client the decision you are forcing them to make is "should I use you or not?". If you provide multiple options, the decision you are encouraging them to make is how to use you.
- Provide transparency – help them understand the activities involved and the costs associated with each activity.
- Demonstrate a cost-conscious attitude – highlight ways in which you have focused on containing costs. This demonstrates that you have empathy for their need to contain costs and that you are finding ways to achieve this to the detriment of your revenue.

This section of the plan should cover:

- Our strategy for justifying why we should be chosen, even if we are more expensive; and
- Our tactics for helping clients understand that the price is fair.

Managing matters

The final section of the pricing strategy focuses on the actions we should be taking during a matter to ensure we maximize the price obtained while satisfying the client. For many practice groups the biggest opportunity to improve pricing performance is to become better at managing scope-creep. Often clients will ask for an estimate at the beginning of a matter, then as things change we fail to update the client. We get to the end of the matter and find we have run well over the estimate and have the choice of writing it off (a financial loss to the firm) or charging the client and potentially damaging the relationship.

If write-offs are an issue for your practice group, start by asking the group what the primary causes of write-offs are. Having identified the primary causes, then brainstorm actions that can be taken to minimize future write-offs. These may include:

- Ensuring a tightly defined scope at the commencement of the matter (note: any price is for an agreed service, not for an infinite work stream);
- More actively monitoring the work performed against the scope to ensure early identification of variations;
- Providing the client with a new agreement for each variation (even if only an email); and
- Keeping clients up-to-date on the costs of matters.

An alternative approach is to jointly agree the actions that should be taken at various stages of a matter. For example:

- Initial client briefing – clarify client goals, determine budget expectations;
- Scoping and pricing – clear scope, identify uncertainties, peer review of pricing;
- Proposal – focus on business impact, provide options;
- Matter management – actively monitor progress against scope and budget;
- Client management – keep the client up-to-date regarding matter status and costs; and
- Post-matter – review with client and identify opportunities to improve.

By focusing on a few key items at each step of a matter, we should be able to minimize write-offs and avoid surprises on invoices.

Conclusion

When pricing is done poorly, it reduces profitability, damages client relationships, and restricts growth opportunities. When pricing is done well, the opposite is achieved – it enables growth, enhances profitability, and strengthens client relationships. Few lawyers have training in contemporary pricing techniques and in a market where clients are becoming increasing focused on containing costs, this creates challenges. Rather than take a passive approach to pricing, I would encourage practice group leaders to actively work with their partners to develop a strategy for achieving improved pricing outcomes. Given that no lever has a greater impact on practice group profitability, shouldn't this be a key item on the practice group's agenda?

The overall objective of the pricing strategy should be to drive profitable growth. This chapter has provided a framework covering:

- Targeting clients and services;
- Setting prices;
- Justifying why we should be chosen, even if we are more expensive; and
- Managing matters.

Having covered each of the above items, the documented pricing strategy will not necessarily cover all the above but rather the key items agreed by the group that will have the most positive impact on improving pricing outcomes. Success of the strategy will be based on implementation, so I encourage you to use the strategy as a living document, regularly reviewed and actioned by the group.

In an increasing competitive market, a successful pricing strategy should help firms win more work, at higher prices, while improving client satisfaction.

Chapter 8:
Focusing your practice team on industry clients

By Patrick J. McKenna, internationally recognized author, lecturer, strategist, and seasoned advisor to the leaders of premier professional service firms

Although the COVID-19 pandemic exposed critical challenges in higher education, the sector has long been ripe for disruption. Nowhere is this more evident than among the nation's business schools. In 2019, a year before the pandemic was on our collective radar, MBA enrollment and applications from students had been in decline for some time and competition for a smaller pool of students was raging among the hundreds of MBA schools across the continent. This rampant marketing and competition for students has raised questions about what a sustainable model for MBA programs might look like.

The generalist MBA, wherein students select a specific discipline – be it finance, operations, or marketing – in which to specialize, is being seen to be outdated such that schools are finding that they increasingly have to differentiate themselves. And finding ways to meaningfully differentiate usually means asking the client – in this case those who hire the end product of graduate education mills – what they need. The response? Increasingly, corporations are expecting their MBA graduates to indeed specialize, but not so much in traditional disciplines as in specific industry sectors – like telecommunication, biotechnology, healthcare, real estate, and so forth.

The world of management education is changing. General programs are not good enough. This shift will mean an end to the conventional "cookie cutter" MBA, where all students learned the same basic business skills. The two-year MBA with some opportunity for industry-specific specialization is becoming the gold standard.

Let's compare what is going on in management education with what is happening in the legal profession. In a US survey of in-house counsel[1] (one of many measuring this factor), when asked *"What most influences your selection of outside law firms?"*, 204 respondents chose as their number one criterion: *"Demonstrated understanding of my business/industry"*. Among the

14 different criteria, this was three times more important than the firm's directory listings or its email communications, and four times more important than social media activity (LinkedIn profile or blogs), or invitations to some sporting event or a meal.

Meanwhile in Australasia, the Beaton Benchmarks Research[2] shows that "firms with the strongest industry reputations are winning more work", and that clients are *"willing to pay more for a firm that demonstrates superior industry experience combined with technical expertise"* (emphasis added). Their research shows that 82 percent of law firm clients have selected a firm that was more expensive than the other options based on their demonstrated industry know-how. This research concludes that *"investing time and effort in developing demonstrable industry expertise across the firm will have a much greater ROI than a lateral hire program"*. And my old friend George Beaton would tell you that these statistics have remained constant for the past ten years!

Today, many firms would assert they have embraced having a smattering of industry groups in their firms. Nevertheless, it is interesting and informative to look at what some of these groups may actually signal to clients about the firm's industry knowledge, seriousness, and competence.

It is not what you call the industry, it is what the client calls itself that is most important

When you think about the various options available for stimulating revenue growth, one of those options is driven by the preponderance of various industries that are located in your particular market footprint.

That said, I am always surprised by the lack of knowledge some professionals display in understanding which industries often have a prevailing influence in their particular locale. In fact, in a number of client meetings (after having done the required homework myself), I've asked partners to tell me, *"What particular industry concentration or 'industry cluster' is your city, state, or region focusing attention and even investing fiscal resources in developing?"* A short period of stunned silence is then often punctuated with some wild guesses and sometimes a few manage to guess correctly.

As a team leader, when you think about industry clusters you might naturally imagine the car manufacturers of Detroit, computer makers of Silicon Valley, aircraft manufacturers of Seattle, financial services in New York, and the movie makers of Hollywood; but industry clusters are more than just a collection of companies in the same industry. Industry clusters are actually a geographical proximate group of interconnected companies with associated institutions in a particular specialization – all linked by networks.

In other words, while some locality can have an industry group, for example the Napa Valley vineyards, what would make this group a cluster would be the presence of upstream and downstream specialists. Using the example of the Napa Valley vineyards, this would include upstream manufacturers and suppliers of herbicides, pesticides, and irrigation, harvesting and processing equipment – while downstream would include manufacturers and suppliers of winemaking equipment, bottles, labels, and corks. The associated institutions would then include government departments (including export), educational and research organizations, plus other related industries like tourism and hospitality.

The challenge that arises from all of this can often manifest itself in clearly understanding what specific industry you are really working in and how you are communicating your expertise and value to the market – especially to prospective clients.

For example, in one particular firm I was engaged in working with, as I examined the various clusters in their New York State market, I noticed that one of the top three industry clusters was "Photonics", which included data transmission technologies, laser processing, and spectroscope analysis. When one examined the firm's website you could not find a single mention of anyone having done work in the "Photonics" industry. When I then raised this point later in our strategy sessions, I was informed that the firm had a long history of serving a number of major companies in the "Optics" industry.

Now, as I diplomatically explained to them, you're welcome to call it the Optics industry, but if I, as the client, call it the Photonics industry and am proud of being an active member of the New York Photonics Industry Association, you might just see how you, your team, and your firm could be perceived to be absolutely inapt!

Meanwhile, by not focusing your attention on the right industry "label" you may have just missed opportunities for leveraging your competence into other closely located geographic areas like Michigan, Colorado, Arizona, Florida, and the Carolinas where there are active Photonics industry clusters. But then I suppose you could always explore the available prospects in New Mexico, on the other side of the country, the only state that I could identify that had an active "Optics" industry cluster. The label you attach to your industry group matters.

As all industries eventually mature, they naturally fracture into multiple sub-industries

Some years back I was engaged to work with a technology industry group to help the partners develop a strategic plan and a direction for growth.

Not too far into what had been scheduled to be an initial four-hour working session, I discerned that four of the partners served software developers, three others focused much of their attention on cable television companies, three were developing expertise with companies in the digital publishing space, and the remaining four spent their professional time working with telecommunication operations clients. Each of these were operating under the same group umbrella ("technology") but were actually sub-groups in entirely different industries. (And I still find the same disconnect within large corporate and large litigation practice groups, comprised of professionals that for the most part, are serving very different kinds of clients.) *News flash: You cannot develop a strategic plan for an industry group if you don't all serve the same kind of clients.*

Today, this same situation is true with numerous industry groups. To be provocative, I would strongly advocate that there is no such thing as a "healthcare lawyer"! One blog post[3] I noticed, which got a fair bit of attention, announced: *"Want to expand? Five Hot Legal Practice Areas to Consider."* It advised lawyers that: *"Changing technology, government policies, and legal environments mean that there are more opportunities than ever to expand your practice into new areas. Here are just a few ideas to get you started."* And number one amongst its hot areas to consider was healthcare.

The way some firms define and describe their industry groups is really quite amusing. If you look at healthcare by way of example, and examine various law firm websites, you are likely to see a description that reads something like this:

> *"We offer clients the advantages of both a concentrated practice in healthcare law and a business firm with broad and varied areas of experience. Our Healthcare practice enjoys an outstanding reputation for its knowledge in health law and its leadership in the health law community. Our strength lies in the ability to understand and keep pace with the numerous changes in the healthcare industry and to work creatively with clients to achieve workable solutions. We offer a comprehensive approach with many inherent advantages. Because we are familiar with how healthcare is delivered and financed, we can respond quickly to the business and financial needs of our healthcare clients and to the practical realities they face. Our experience encompasses a wide range of matters of concern to the healthcare industry, including:*
>
> - *Business transactions;*
> - *Integrated delivery systems;*

- *Contracts;*
- *Managed care relationships;*
- *Healthcare provider financing;*
- *Restructuring and reorganization;*
- *Tax advice for tax-exempt and for-profit entities;*
- *Antitrust;*
- *Fraud and abuse;*
- *Medicare, Medicaid, and third party reimbursement;*
- *Employment issues;*
- *Credentialing and accreditation;*
- *Certificate of need;*
- *Patient care and operational issues; and*
- *Medical malpractice."*

It sounds both comprehensive and convincing. The only small problem from any client's perspective is that Healthcare, as an industry, has fractured into numerous (well over 44) distinct sub-industries (witness my earlier example with technology) as it has grown and matured, each of which is composed of companies that believe they are very unique.

So, if you happen to be a prospective client operating as an ambulatory service, general medical and surgical hospital, family planning clinic or dental equipment and supplies company, there is no indication in the aforementioned website description that this particular healthcare industry group has any experience whatsoever in handling your kind of business. Beyond those obvious sub-industries there are also numerous micro-niches that could provide lucrative opportunities for those lawyers desiring to specialize and effectively market that specific expertise to become the go-to providers and achieve a significant strategic advantage over those attorneys who simply claim healthcare experience.

If this doesn't make sense for any reason, let's consider the industry of professional services and a sub-industry known as the legal profession. If some service provider held themselves out to be the renowned expert in professional service firms, your first question would be, "Yes, that's fine, but what do you specifically know about law firms?" Then if that same renowned expert began to tell you about how they employed their smarts in marketing to the advantage of some major accounting firm, even though you might admit that the tactics were equally applicable, you would still inquire as to what experience they have had serving a law firm – like yours. You reject any notion that being an expert in an industry as broad as professional services, or even marketing leadership in the accounting sector, is sufficient. I will never forget one Georgia-based firm even going so far as to acknowledge that I had worked with many law firms, but *"Had I had ever served any firms in the Deep South?"*

Isn't it fascinating how the mindset we bring to the table as purchasers of professional services is so completely different from the mindset we exhibit as sellers of professional services?

Perhaps one more illustrative example. As it happens, I sit on the board of what in Western Canada has become one of the leading groups of private medical clinics in the anti-aging and regenerative medicine niche (it is interesting to witness how anti-aging has become more fascinating to me with each passing year). Anyway, the CEO was facing a potential litigation threat, looking for some risk assessment and preventative guidance, and therefore invited the leading lawyers from three different law firms' healthcare groups in for a brief meet-and-greet.

The first two lawyers from one firm entered the boardroom and after a few minutes of social chit-chat the CEO asked, *"So, tell me please, what do you know about BHRT?"* The two lawyers exchanged glances and one said, *"Forgive us as I'm not sure we understand that acronym"*. The CEO responded, *"It stands for Bio-identical Hormone Replacement Therapy"*. The faces of the two attorneys now showed a touch of distress until one offered, *"I'm not certain precisely how much experience we have had in that particular area, but we are the largest Healthcare practice in the country and I'm certain that we would be up-to-speed in no time."*

The CEO's reaction: *"Thanks for coming in."*

As sellers, we appear to be quite content with telling the marketplace that we are healthcare lawyers with little regard for what our clients are looking to buy. And in this instance the healthcare industry is fragmented into dozens of sub-industries. Therefore, those lawyers who develop a specific expertise in micro-niche areas like personalized DNA-based medicine, mobile health appliances, stem-cell applications, e-health information systems, or lithotripsy services, and then effectively market that specific expertise will become the go-to providers and achieve a significant strategic advantage over those other attorneys who simply claim to be healthcare lawyers. In most industries you need to be very specific about the sub-industry that you are targeting to serve.

There are some areas of opportunity that initially defy simple industry categorization

One particular area of emerging opportunity is in what is being categorized the "Internet of Things" or IoT. Most often, we hear about IoT in the context of wearable devices – things like the Fitbit that promise to improve health and wellness, or more fully featured devices like the Apple Watch and Google Glasses that also extend such smartphone functions as messaging or Web searching. But while consumer technology is a hot area, IoT will likely have a far greater impact in manufacturing, resources and energy, utilities, and civic services.

Simply defined, IoT is about connecting objects, from trucks to refrigerators and hydro meters, to the internet. Data gleaned from the sensors and systems applied to these objects can then be used to monitor, control, or redesign business processes and so will likely impact numerous industries.

Meanwhile, a number of IoT focused venture funds have been launched and, globally, every few weeks there is either an acquisition or a new company starting up. According to Accenture,[4] roughly three-quarters of large companies are investing 20 percent of their research and development spending on big data and analytics, which IoT is driving.

My research into this area of opportunity indicates that there are four expanding segments – makers and installers of physical sensors, connection providers (landline, wireless, telecoms, etc.), storage and security hardware and software (server farms, the cloud) to hold on to and encrypt all the collected data, and finally the data analysis software. Some companies do all that in one solution; others focus on one piece of the spectrum.

The projections for growth are huge; networking equipment titan Cisco Systems Inc. believes IoT represents a $19 trillion (US) global market and predicts that 50 billion devices will be connected to the Internet this year.[5]

So, is there a law firm reading this that will be the first to launch an IoT Focus Team – or are you content to let the Big Four competitors occupy this lucrative market space? In spite of what some pundits might suggest, growth is not dead; it is merely hiding amongst areas of opportunity not easily categorized within traditional legal practice group or departmental structures.

Industry sector expertise is a key differentiator

For those who missed one particular development that emerged a few years back, 750-attorney Husch Blackwell, a St Louis based firm, completely dispensed with its traditional practice group structure in favor of organizing itself into a configuration of only industry groups. Firm chairman, Maurice Watson, explained to this author:

> *"We were aware that the competition, especially in our segment of the market, was intensifying, that there were too many talented lawyers and talented firms and too little great work to be had. As a consequence, there's much greater pressure and focus on the need for law firms to be able to differentiate themselves as well as establish, for clients, that they can offer some kind of additional value that other comparable firms could not provide."*

Back in 1989, I happened to co-author what I believe was the very first book[6] on the marketing (and we were not allowed to use that word back in those days) of legal services (for Butterworths Publishing and distributed internationally), wherein I confidently predicted that within ten years every significant law firm would be structured based on industry groups. So much for the complete folly of making predictions!

Fast forward over three decades and it is still staggering for me to understand why, in spite of decades of witnessing other professions (like our brethren in the accounting and management consulting fields) focus on seeing client need through an industry lens, so many law firms still miss this opportunity. It gets even crazier when we consider the research in the recently published *Future Ready Lawyer Survey: Performance Driver*[7] and evidence that one of the primary reasons for corporate counsel to either select (or deselect) any firm is increasingly based on the degree to which that firm clearly "demonstrates" an understanding of the client's business, their industry, and what specialized issues are of paramount importance.

What makes industry sector expertise a meaningful differentiator?

First, where you enter into serving a specific industry segment and are eventually perceived by the sub-industry members as having specialized knowledge in their unique business and legal matters (*"you talk their lingo"*), you can develop a name recognition that becomes hard for others to match.

Second, in any market with a steep learning curve, being first to target and develop a presence in some specific industry segment (think: synthetic biology) can confer the advantage of having a head start. That head start allows you to position yourself as a primary source for media commentary, for seminar presentations, for having articles published, and other such positioning tactics.

Finally, by being early and effective in targeting some lucrative sub-industry, you have the opportunity to draw clients into your web, creating "switching costs" that deter those clients from any notion of later moving their work to other follow-the-leader law firms.

Your future personal growth and career prosperity may very well depend upon you participating actively and continuously investing to build your knowledge and skills within some chosen industry segment, and then working diligently to establish a significant presence.

References

1. Further information may be obtained by contacting Michael Rynowecer – BTI Consulting Group, https://bticonsulting.com.
2. Further information may be obtained from contacting Dr George Beaton, www.beatonglobal.com/market-insights.
3. www.findlaw.com/legalblogs/strategist/want-to-expand-5-hot-practice-areas-to-consider-for-2015
4. www.accenture.com/_acnmedia/pdf-44/accenture-iot-platforms-web.pdf
5. www.forbes.com/sites/moorinsights/2016/02/08/is-cisco-systems-the-one-to-beat-in-iot/?sh=341dafcb1443
6. *Practice Development: Creating A Marketing Mindset*, Butterworth-Heinemann (1989).
7. www.globenewswire.com/fr/news-release/2020/06/04/2043524/0/en/2020-Wolters-Kluwer-Future-Ready-Lawyer-Performance-Drivers-and-Change-in-the-Legal-Sector.html

Chapter 9:
Implementing the balanced scorecard at the practice group level

By John Sterling, founding partner, Sterling Strategies, LLC

The balanced scorecard – an overview of Kaplan and Norton's system

Robert Kaplan and David Norton introduced the concept of a balanced scorecard in a *Harvard Business Review* article in January 1992. The concept was based on research Norton had done as a practice leader at KPMG. The research continued and the concept was fully fleshed out in the pair's 1996 book *The Balanced Scorecard: Translating Strategy into Action.*[1]

As presented in the book (and subsequently through numerous articles and a continuing consultancy), the balanced scorecard is a management system (i.e. a management tool) designed to connect higher level, longer range strategy to day-to-day implementation. Hence the subtitle of the book – *Translating Strategy into Action.*

Most readers are familiar with at least one of Kaplan and Norton's intentions relative to bringing greater balance to strategic management. Namely, the authors wanted to add non-financial objectives and measures to a management environment dominated by financial accounting measures – thereby adding balance to the mix of measures. However, the authors sought to bring greater balance in two other respects as well. First, Kaplan and Norton believed that the continuing reliance on financial accounting measures led to an inordinately internal focus at most organizations. Second, they believed that measures needed to provide a balance of objective, quantitative metrics and subjective, qualitative measures. As strategic management professionals, the authors recognized that some goals and objectives are expressed more effectively in qualitative terms, and are simply more inspirational and understandable in those terms.

Ultimately, the authors were strong believers in the management truism "not measured, not managed" (a concept coined by Tom DeMarco at Bell Labs).[2] To that truism they added the notion that measures should be balanced in terms of their external and internal focus, their financial and non-financial aspects, and between quantitative and qualitative considerations.

The balanced scorecard in its most basic form

The balanced scorecard includes four inter-related considerations in its most basic form (see Figure 1). All of those considerations flow from a central driving force – the overarching vision and strategy of the organization.

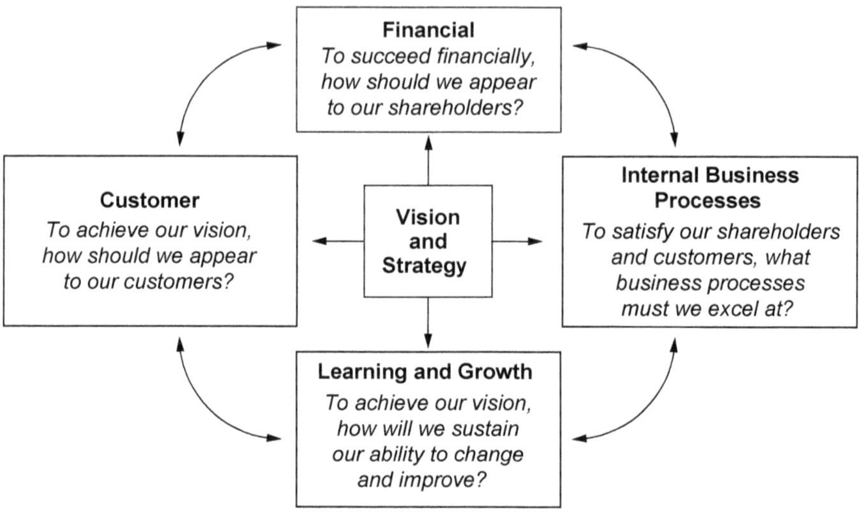

Figure 1: The balanced scorecard. Source: Kaplan and Norton.

Financial perspective

This dimension measures the organization in the context of what it should deliver to shareholders through the achievement of its vision and strategy. It should be noted that Kaplan and Norton developed the balanced scorecard on the presumption that shareholders were essentially financial investors – not partners in a law firm.

Customer perspective

This dimension considers what the organization needs to deliver to its customers to maintain their business over the near and long run. Kaplan and Norton strongly emphasized the importance of defining what customers (or market segment) a business serves. Measuring a business' success in meeting and exceeding the needs of customers requires the business to know who its customers are. Critically, it implies a solid understanding of customers' priorities and expectations.

Internal business process perspective

The third dimension flows from the first two. It focuses attention on business processes that are most critical to satisfying customers and/or to driving shareholder value. Kaplan and Norton intended to motivate readers to move beyond standalone process improvement initiatives (for example, re-engineering, total quality management, etc.) and to focus on developing and/or improving processes that really impact customer satisfaction and/or financial performance.

Learning and growth

The final dimension focuses on ensuring that people have the knowledge and tools necessary to achieve the vision and strategy. It presumes that, in a knowledge-based economy, the workforce will need to get smarter over time, will need to enhance their capabilities, and will employ technology and systems to improve their performance.

Because Kaplan and Norton developed the balanced scorecard with the intention of creating an integrated strategic management system, they advocated approaching the scorecard in what they considered to be a logical order. That logical progression presumes that articulating a vision and developing corporate strategy is a top-down endeavor. The balanced scorecard is an integrated tool that translates that top-down strategy into terms that the rest of the organization can understand and to which individuals can respond.

In other words, it is assumed that the organization has a vision and strategy – and that the balanced scorecard will provide a mechanism for translating that strategy into day-to-day implementation. The balanced scorecard provides a framework for adopting implementation action plans and related measures that drive strategy implementation.

With vision and strategy in hand, senior management can articulate and refine financial objectives. In addition, senior management can develop consensus regarding target markets and goals related to customers and market segments. The business process aspect of the scorecard should be informed by a clear understanding of financial and customer objectives. Likewise, people and capability driven aspects of the scorecard only make sense in the context of the first three dimensions (i.e., knowledge development should be focused on things that drive process improvement, customer needs, and financial performance).

The balanced scorecard as a management tool

Kaplan and Norton envisioned organizations adopting the balanced scorecard as an integrated management tool. This approach implies that an organization will deploy the system via a cascading process – starting from senior management and ultimately involving the entire organization in implementation. Thus, effective use of a balanced scorecard essentially means getting a broad cross-section of people directly involved in strategy implementation.

Kaplan and Norton's recommended approach for managing this high involvement, cascading process is summarized in Figure 2 and is outlined in the following points.

Vision and strategy

Vision statements are generally short and compelling. Some criticize them as "motherhood and apple pie" – meaning they say things no one could disagree with. In their original research, Kaplan and Norton found that there was a degree of truth to this criticism. Specifically, what the authors found was that senior management was often in lock-step agreement on statements of high-level vision and strategy. However, when asked to translate that high-level strategy into objectives relative to shareholder and/or customer needs and expectations, there was wide divergence. Executives agreed superficially on the strategy, but had not translated that agreement into more specific objectives.

Figure 2: Approach for managing balanced scorecards. Source: Kaplan and Norton.

Thus, the first step in implementing an integrated, cascading approach to strategy implementation (i.e. the balanced scorecard approach) is ensuring that senior management can explain the strategy in terms the organization can understand. That generally means translating the higher level strategy into:

- Three- to five-year financial and customer objectives;
- An identification of the business processes most critical to achieving the financial and customer objectives – along with high level objectives for performance improvement in those processes; and
- An identification of the critical organizational capabilities needed to achieve the financial, customer, and process improvement objectives.

In addition to positioning the organization to engage people directly in strategy implementation, Kaplan and Norton note that the process of translating the higher level strategy into these more concrete terms leads the senior management team towards stronger consensus and harmony.

Communicating and linking

The next step in the cascading process involves linking the high-level objectives to the day-to-day responsibilities of people throughout the organization. It is largely a process of answering the question "What does this strategy mean to me?" for every person involved in strategy implementation. That implies effective communication deep into the organization.

Ideally, this communication process should be framed as a dialogue. While the strategy and objectives are essentially being delivered from the top down, a deep understanding of "what it means for me" is something that is best understood via discussion. Broad involvement in strategy development leads to better implementation because understanding and buy-in are established deeply within the organization. This communication and linkage step is about building understanding deep within the organization.

Kaplan and Norton recommend creating linkages in at least two ways. First, functional areas can identify the corporate level objectives most meaningful to their day-to-day responsibilities (for example, customers, business processes, organizational support functions, etc.). Those higher-level objectives can then be broken down and linked to activities in each functional area. Second, rewards can be linked to performance on those functional level metrics.

Planning and target setting

The third step in this cascading process involves planning the work and setting meaningful, time-based targets. At its core, this step closely resembles a planning process widely used by large organizations in the 1970s and 1980s – management by objectives. The process essentially involves two critical steps:

- Development of and agreement on action plans at the functional area level – including identification of the initiatives to be carried out, individuals to be involved in execution of the initiatives, and significant milestones for each initiative; and
- Development of a related set of nearer term, small-scale targets to be used as measures for progress.

This "planning and targeting" step is ultimately designed to move the organization and its people from long-term to short-term thinking. By directly engaging people in action planning and setting near-term targets, the organization helps people focus on what is truly important and strategic. Further, it helps them to relate their day-to-day work to the long-range vision and strategy of the organization.

Finally, this step provides the context for aligning resources with both the long-range strategy and near-term action plans. Thus, Kaplan and Norton recommend integrating the budgeting process into this step of balanced scorecard development.

Strategic feedback and learning

The final step in the process is feedback to senior management. If the first three steps are about a top-down cascading of planning and goal setting, the final step is about cycling the information gained via implementation back to the senior management team. Kaplan and Norton characterize this final step as *"organizational learning at the senior management level"*.

The feedback should be more than simply a review of how the organization is doing in implementing the strategy. Critically, it should also address the question of whether underlying assumptions – about the market, competitors, customer needs, organizational lynchpins – are proving themselves true. Many organizations identify external indicators that link to key market assumptions undergirding their strategy – and monitor those indicators to ensure the organization is not surprised by changing market conditions that undermine the strategy.

In truth, a well-developed balanced scorecard is quite explicit in identifying key assumptions. This is true with regard to assumptions driving financial expectations and external market conditions (including customer needs). Likewise, it is true with regard to internal assumptions. The process is intended to drive the management team (at each level of the organization) to think about cause and effect relationships. For instance, the selection of internal business processes on which to focus is a function of identifying processes believed to be connected to customer needs and financial performance. In turn, the development of action plans and targets associated with improving those processes is a function of assumptions regarding underlying performance drivers for those processes.

This final step is an opportunity to engage the organization in strategy review. In answering the questions "What is working?" and "What is not working?" the organization is not really engaging in performance appraisal. Rather, it is evaluating the cause and effect assumptions within the balanced scorecard. It provides a unique and powerful opportunity for the senior management team to assess the validity and potential of the vision and strategy it is leading.

To the extent the strategy remains on course, the loop repeats itself and the organization is once again engaged in the process of cascading long-term objectives into near-term actions and targets. To the extent the strategy is off course, senior management is compelled to return to fundamental assumptions and the vision it has set. The cycle should not be re-engaged if the strategy is genuinely off course.

Implementing the balanced scorecard at the practice group level – a "how to" primer

Planning a balanced scorecard development at the practice group level is considerably less complex than doing so at the firm level. Nevertheless, a generic process such as that outlined below will prove to be inadequate if implementation of the process is not customized and tailored to the practice. Customization will be needed to ensure the process is:

- Responsive;
- Fact based; and
- Inclusive.

The recommended practice-level approach to strategy and balanced scorecard development includes a streamlined five-phase approach:

- Information gathering and background analysis;
- Vision and strategic plan development;
- High-level objective setting;
- Action planning and balanced scorecard development; and
- Dialogue, evaluation, and adjustment.

Each of the five respective phases is discussed in the following sections.

Information gathering and background analysis

Like firm-level strategic plans, practice plans should be built on a foundation of well-informed background analyses. Input and information should be gathered from a diverse set of sources. Data gathering is generally less extensive, but can include the same types of sources used in firm-level planning:

- The firm's financial system – which can generally provide valuable information regarding the practice's financial performance at multiple levels (practice group, client, individual lawyer, etc.);
- The partners within the practice, as well as firm leaders and partners in complementary and/or inbound and outbound referring practices;
- The practice's other lawyers – especially in this era of highly mobile professionals;
- Competitive benchmarking reports – such as the PricewaterhouseCoopers, Peer Monitor, and Citigroup financial benchmarking surveys;
- Secondary market research literature – including profiles of competitors, rankings and ratings by general counsel and third party rating firms, and other trend line articles and monographs;
- Clients (including lapsed and prospective clients) – who can provide some of the most valuable insights regarding the practice's competitive position and its strengths and weaknesses; and
- Chambers of Commerce and government agencies – for data on economic and regulatory trends.

In turn, that raw data and information needs to be analyzed, so the practice group can put it to work in a productive decision-making context. While analyses will vary based on the firm and will likely be more direct than firm-level analyses, worthwhile analyses in preparation for practice-level strategic planning can still include:

- A systematic assessment of strengths, weaknesses, opportunities, and threats (SWOT analysis);
- A review of competitive intensity (Michael Porter's "five forces" analysis)[3];
- A systematic review of political, economic, social, technological, environmental, and legal trends (PESTEL analysis);
- Analysis of competitive positioning both among clients (built on client input, competitive profiles, and benchmarking data), as well as among professionals (since competition for good people has become fiercer than competition for clients in many markets); and
- Financial analyses (highlighting where the practice group derives the bulk of its profitability).

Ideally, the background information-gathering and related analyses should be summarized into a consolidated list of the most significant strategic issues facing the practice. Generally, a good summary can boil down all the analyses to fewer than ten major strategic issues. The issues can then be framed as fundamental questions to be answered via the development of the strategic plan and the related balanced scorecard.

Vision and strategic plan development

In the absence of firm-level direction vis-à-vis the role a practice is expected to play within the firm, it is reasonable for a practice group to develop a mini version of a one-page strategic plan.

A mini strategic plan at the practice level can be created so that it fits on a single page. Like a firm-level plan, a practice's vision and strategy should come from the lawyers who lead the practice – directly via their management roles and indirectly via outsized professional contributions. The work can be done by an ad hoc committee – or, if the group is compact enough, by all partners or all lawyers in the practice. The strategic plan at the practice level would include a similar set of three fairly high-level elements to those outlined for the firm.

Mission

A statement of overall strategic direction that includes:

- A clear vision for the future of the law practice (i.e. what the practice aspires to be over the long run);
- A direct articulation of *core purpose* (i.e. what the practice intends to deliver on behalf of its core stakeholders – clients, shareholders, employees, the firm as a whole); and
- A brief statement of *core values* (i.e. those few immutable cultural beliefs that bind the practice to the firm and in turn that bind the firm together).

Primary excellence goals

A limited number of very high-level positioning statements that articulate where the practice intends to concentrate its resources in order to excel.

- Like firm-level goals, most practice-level primary excellence goals respond to competitive pressures and the need to excel in selected areas in order to remain competitively strong (i.e. they are not necessarily unique to the firm or practice, but rather are areas where the practice must be excellent in order to remain competitive);
- At least one (and ideally more) primary excellence goal should focus on developing a superior market position in an area (or areas) that will genuinely distinguish the practice in the competitive marketplace; and
- A central guiding principle in identifying and articulating primary excellence goals is to ensure that each goal focuses the practice on excelling in areas that determine the outcome of competition in the marketplace (i.e. that matter to clients and to people – the two areas where the practice faces continuing competition).

High-level strategies

An articulation of what the practice will do to achieve the primary excellence goals (i.e. an articulation of resource allocation priorities vis-à-vis each of the goals). Done right, high-level strategies bring clarity to the goals. Read together, the primary excellence goals and strategies provide clarity with regard to the practice's strategic priorities. A one-page strategic plan developed with these basic guidelines can take the structure depicted in Figure 3.

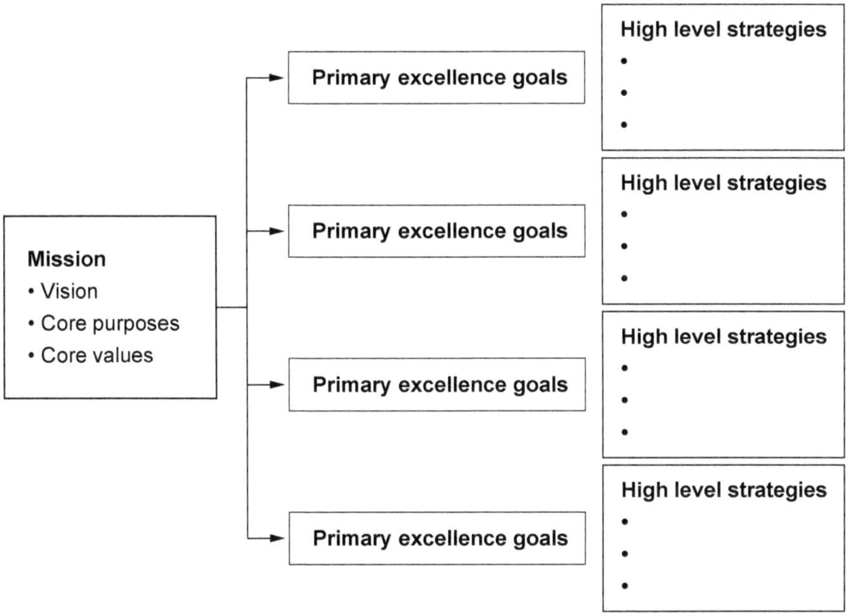

Figure 3: Generic one-page strategic plan.

High-level objective setting

The next phase of a practice-level planning process involves translating the strategic plan into high-level objectives related to the first two dimensions of the balanced scorecard – financial and client relationship. The high-level objective for the financial dimension at the practice level may boil down to profits per equity partner. However, practices may adopt high-level objectives related to other profit drivers (for example, leverage, revenue per lawyer, relative competitive rates, realization, profit margin, etc.).

The high-level objective for the client relationship dimension will vary from practice to practice. Because the primary excellence goals have focused on competitive positioning, it should be a relatively straightforward process to select one or two high-level objectives for client relationships – objectives that quantify what the practice looks like to clients in the context of the market positioning called for in the primary excellence goals.

Setting these first two high-level objectives at the practice level positions the planning team to begin the cascading process called for in Kaplan and Norton's strategic mapping and balanced scorecard methodologies. Essentially, from this point forward, the practice group can pursue balanced scorecard development "by the book".

Action planning and balanced scorecard development

Because the planning work has occurred entirely at the practice group level in this process, there is no need to engage in portfolio analysis and mapping. The practice group can move directly into the more traditional strategy mapping and balanced scorecard development process Kaplan and Norton recommend vis-à-vis the four dimensions of the scorecard. As discussed earlier in this chapter, that process involves getting a substantial cross-section of people within the practice group to develop action plans, milestones, metrics, and accountabilities associated with the practice-level vision and strategy. This should include any individual practice development planning partners and other lawyers are expected to develop (usually on an annualized basis).

The process requires the practice-level planning team to build a strategy map related to each of the balanced scorecard dimensions, but tailored to the specific requirements and focus of the practice group.

Dialogue, evaluation, and adjustment

Once the strategy is in place at practice level and the balanced scorecards and related action plans are operational, the process turns to dialogue and feedback. These allow the iterative improvement that is at the heart of the value of the balanced scorecard.

The practice group's balanced scorecards provide the basis for dialogue and feedback, allowing the practice to pursue action plans with clear milestones and expectations for particular outcomes relative to financial performance, client relationships, and professional capabilities. With specific, achievable milestones set out, the practice will be able to measure its progress – or otherwise – over time.

Depending upon the practice group and its role in the firm's strategy, practice leadership should plan to evaluate progress anywhere from two to four times over the course of the year. Practice leadership should also plan to engage in a dialogue regarding strategic progress with firm management as well. Those review sessions provide an opportunity for ongoing dialogue – keeping the practice on track and ensuring the firm is in sync with the direction the practice is pursuing and the results the practice is achieving.

On an annual basis, the practice can assess progress against its high level objectives – financial, client relationship, and people related. In addition, practice leadership can make necessary adjustments in the overall strategy as well as a straightforward update of the action plans, priorities, and related scorecards at the practice level.[4]

References

1. Kaplan, R., and Norton, D., *The Balanced Scorecard*, Boston: Harvard Business Press, 1996.
2. *Controlling Software Projects: Management, Measurement and Estimation*; Yourdon Press, 1982.
3. Porter, M., 'How competitive forces shape strategy', Harvard Business Review, March/April 1979.
4. This chapter is based on edited extracts from Sterling, J. *Balanced Scorecards for Law Firms*, London: Ark Group, 2009.

Chapter 10:
Coaching for practice group leaders

By Hannah Beko, lawyer, author, and founder of Authentically Speaking, a coaching and training consultancy to the legal profession

In this chapter, we will consider the difference between a high-performing practice group leader comfortable in adopting an authentic, open, and coaching-based leadership style versus the more managerial/directive approach traditionally taken in law.

It is noteworthy that at the start of the global pandemic, when many workforces were sent home to work, often for the first time, leaders believed they would require a strong dictatorial management style to retain control over their people. The reality was the complete opposite. Firms found that their attorneys were on the whole working longer hours than ever. Without the commute to break up their day, more time was available to work. There was also a fear culture around what the future might hold, whether it would require a doubly strong work ethic to demonstrate commitment and value to the firm, ensuring they would be retained in what we all expected to be a challenging market environment.

If the legal profession wasn't already in need of a change in the style and effectiveness of its leadership, the past few years have shown how vital this will be to attract and retain the best talent within practice groups and produce the highest quality work for clients.

My research for this chapter began with a series of interviews with practice group leaders and a global L&D lead into what differentiates a mediocre practice group leader from an excellent one, and why it matters to the firm.

The fundamental difference that came across in these interviews was mindset. Although we will break this down into several connected issues, what creates standout practice group leaders seems to be a willingness (or perhaps the courage) to shift their mindset from attorney to leader. It is widely understood that few firms offer effective managerial training to attorneys. Frequently one will be promoted due to a combination of billings, client relationships, "face fits", or occasionally through necessity.

Research published in September 2021 by LawCare,[1] the UK-based charity supporting mental health and wellbeing in the legal profession for the past 25 years, found that only 47.6 percent of those in a management or supervisory role had received any leadership or management training, but of those who had, 89.4 percent said it was helpful or very helpful. I conducted my own LinkedIn poll at the time of writing, and 61 percent said that they had not had any specific training.

Mindset matters

We have already seen in chapter two of this book the importance of mindset in handling change, and the adoption of a servant-leader mindset. Being flexible, adaptable, and open to change is not something the attorney mindset traditionally embraces. The idea of a servant-leader encourages prioritizing the whole over the one, again not customarily encouraged within the practice of law.

Psychologist Carol Dweck says:

> *"Much of what we think we understand of our personality comes from our mindset. This both propels us and prevents us from fulfilling our potential."*[2]

In *A Summary of Fixed and Growth Mindsets*, it is noted that:

> *"Dweck's work shows the power of our most basic beliefs. Whether conscious or subconscious, they strongly 'affect what we want and whether we succeed in getting it'. Much of what we think we understand of our personality comes from our 'mindset'."*[3]

Widely considered the leading authority in the distinction of a fixed versus a growth mindset, Dweck highlights that those with a fixed mindset tend to be less able to develop their skills beyond certain self-determined expectations.

The following "fixed mindset" traits can be seen relatively frequently inside our profession:

- Feeling our position may be threatened by others with the same (or greater) perceived ability, resulting in a reluctance to support the growth and development of our people;
- Avoiding situations where we do not consider ourselves the expert in the room for fear of showing weakness or lack of knowledge, including avoiding cases or matters where we do not consider ourselves an authority;

- Being uncomfortable about receiving feedback, especially of the constructive or negative variety, even actively avoiding situations where feedback may be given;
- Feeling a need to "look like" the most experienced professional, perceptions being of greater importance perhaps than the reality; and
- A lack of trust in our team, resulting in a need for a micromanaging mentality for fear that people will not perform without directive management.

In the alternative, a "growth" mindset can be characterized by these attributes in attorneys:

- Actively promoting the success and achievement of those within our teams and taking every opportunity to learn from others;
- Seeking out learning opportunities, being unafraid to be the "newbie" in the room, and pioneering new approaches in our cases or matters despite the risks of failure or "getting it wrong";
- Embracing feedback when offered, asking for it regularly, and taking on board suggestions with humility and self-reflection as a basis for improvement;
- Setting aside a need to "appear" the expert in favour of focusing on the continuing journey of learning, adaptation, and change; and
- Being comfortable with high levels of trust within our groups, promoting autonomy and initiative wherever possible.

Why do practice group leaders with a growth mindset stand out amongst their peers?

First and foremost, before they were leaders, they were lawyers. Before rising through the ranks of leadership, these individuals had become experts in their own discipline. Stepping into a leadership role at the practice group level involves a significant abandonment of their prior roles and responsibilities.

Trevor Sterling, senior partner and head of the major trauma group at Moore Barlow, says, *"It is important to stay on the tools to some degree in order to manage your team"*.[4]

While retaining a level of client-facing work is always ideal so that they remain grounded and fully aware of the pressures their teams face, those who do not break away from a substantially fee earning role do not fully embrace all that it means to be an effective practice group leader. Taking this step involves finding themselves in unchartered territory. Or if they don't make the leap and remain instead in their "safe zone", they don't grow into the effective leaders they could be.

Adrian Barker, global L&D manager and executive coach at Freshfields Bruckhaus Deringer, shared with me[5] his thoughts on the difference between embracing the mindset shift required as opposed to remaining on the safer side:

> *"Practice group leaders have the potential to be incredibly powerful. Some choose to wield that power and some do not. There are those who drive excellence and others remain lawyers who are tinkering at leadership."*

If a growth mindset and becoming a business manager first and lawyer second is such a large component of excellence at this level, what prevents some leaders from making this shift?

In much of my work with the legal profession over the past few years, I've come to see just how much of our collective behaviours are driven by fear. Although ironically, the outside world might find this a surprising concept, fear is not commonly attributed to the archetypal lawyer. Yet when you consider the extraordinarily long hours worked, agreeing to clients' (frequently unreasonable) demands, and lack of care for one's own health and wellbeing in the pursuit of achievement and status, you do have to ask why.

Although you can find references going back to biblical scriptures, world-renowned author, coach, speaker, and philanthropist Tony Robbins says of fear:

> *"Fear of failure, fear of rejection or fear that we're just not enough – fear is a common current that runs through all of our lives. And if we let it, fear can keep us locked up in the prison of the comfortable and predictable, which prevents us from reaching our true potential."*[6]

Fear has driven human behaviour since the beginning of our existence. Fear kept us alive in the early years of humankind when as cave people we might be attacked by lions and tigers. The fear of being judged, disliked, and ostracised from our peer group is still a powerful driver.

For some practice group leaders, the fear of moving from the comfort zone of the known, of where they stand easily in their expertise, and instead into a role that involves challenging themselves to grow and develop outside of their safety net of the actual practice of law and to make decisions that might not be popular for the good of the many, is a stage too far. These leaders then remain firmly planted in their fee earner practising attorney role, dabbling in a bit of leadership when absolutely necessary.

Adrian Barker explains:

> *"Some are fearful of getting it wrong, of making a mistake and losing credibility. People at that level exist on their reputation and any chance of that being damaged, is a big risk. There is an underappreciation of just what a large and all-encompassing task leading and managing is."*[7]

For existing and aspiring practice group leaders to step out of the fear and towards excellence therefore requires a deep level of self-reflection as to how they see themselves both as a practising attorney, and in their role as a group leader. In their legal work they may have largely worked alone and whilst the interests of their clients always drove them, it was a case of looking out for number one first and foremost. Truly embracing leadership means shifting from a mindset of one to many. It encompasses shifting from a directive management style that can stifle innovation and engagement to a more open, trusting, and autonomous environment for our groups to thrive.

Coaching questions encouraging self-reflection

Consider how you see yourself as a practising attorney. How comfortable do you feel in this position as opposed to your roles and responsibilities as a practice group leader?

Do you notice any feelings of imposter syndrome, any sense that you are not quite good enough for the role of leader, that the mask may slip at any time, and someone will discover that you are not as good as they think you are?

How supportive are you of other leaders reporting to you inside your group? Internally do you fear that their progression or achievements might somehow damage your career prospects or your reputation?

Do you consider yourself to have a fixed or a growth mindset in your career arena? Note: we can have a growth mindset in certain areas of our life, such as our personal development but find that we have a fixed mindset around our health or our finances, for example. If you find yourself dealing in absolutes such as "I never", "I couldn't", "That wouldn't work for me", "I don't like" etc., then you may have a bit of a fixed mindset around that topic.

If you notice some fear around failure, making a mistake, being judged, make a note of this realization. Realization is half of the battle. Consider how you could replace this belief with something more empowering over time; what else could you believe would help you feel more genuinely confident within your role?

Consider where you adopt a more directional hands-on management style and where you could instead lead with trust and give greater autonomy to your team. Is there room for a more significant shift towards the latter?

What attributes create a great practice group leader?

Let's look at some key attributes of an effective practice group leader, and how these can be cultivated.

High levels of self-awareness around strengths and areas for improvement

> *"Self-awareness seems to have become the latest management buzzword – and for good reason. Research suggests that when we see ourselves clearly, we are more confident and more creative. We make sounder decisions, build stronger relationships, and communicate more effectively. And we're more-effective leaders with more-satisfied employees and more-profitable companies."*[8]

As we have seen, attorneys can find themselves, often unwittingly, trapped by a need to be liked, a need to conform to a certain stereotypical lawyer. Those leaders who stand out are not afraid to examine their own thoughts, feelings, and fears. They will push themselves out of their comfort zone not hindered by a fear of judgement. Similarly, they are not afraid to reach out for help and support from others and don't operate as a lone wolf.

One of the most effective ways to develop your self-awareness skills is to take constructive feedback from those around you. As attorneys move into positions of higher leadership, there can be a tendency to be less and less open to seeking out and listening to feedback. It is also key that such leaders create an environment of openness and honesty if their team are going to bring truthful and valuable feedback without fear of it impacting their own career prospects.

Idea: Arrange some confidential one-to-one discussions with key members of your group and conduct an honest appraisal of the extent to which feedback is being provided to you as leader and check in that you are adopting any changes required as a result.

Ability to create loyalty, goodwill and a sense of being valued

> *"Employees who feel valued are more likely to report better physical and mental health, as well as higher levels of engagement, satisfaction and motivation… Almost all employees (93 percent) who reported feeling valued said that they are motivated to do their best at work and 88 percent reported feeling engaged. This compares to just 33 percent and 38 percent, respectively, of those who said they do not feel valued."*[9]

"Psychological safety" inside our workplace teams is an idea first discussed by Amy Edmondson,[10] a professor at Harvard University. Whilst the term is relatively new, it is rightly gaining traction inside working environments. The human need for "safety" is considered a basic need for the purposes of Maslow's hierarchy of needs (Abraham Maslow first discussed this in his 1943 paper "A Theory of Human Motivation").[11] Historically, law offices have not perhaps paid much attention, if any, to the psychological safety of their employees. Indeed, it would be seen as a weakness and a sign of not being fit for the profession if someone raised such issues. Thankfully for the sake of mental health and wellbeing, but also for the better performance and engagement of staff, attitudes are beginning to change. An effective practice group leader knows this and is mindful of the environment created in their teams.

Says Trish McLellan, director of research and engagement at LawCare:

> *"From a risk management point of view, it's just not appropriate for environments to be so psychologically unsafe that people are terrified to admit a mistake."*[12]

Idea: Creating loyalty, goodwill, and safety require a high level of trust. The effective group leader realises that trust is a two-way street and for them to receive the trust of their group, they must also demonstrate that they trust their team by effective delegation and honest sharing of views and ideas as often as possible.

Embraces learning and development of self and others

Adrian Barker[13] shared his thoughts on those leaders who are always open to learning and development and how these will generally be the most successful at attracting talent to join their team. He said:

> *"Through trainings I have delivered over the past few years I've heard first hand from newer entrants to the profession (and those who train and supervise them) just how highly they value development, learning opportunities, and access to challenging work, giving them more potential to grow and discover their own strengths."*
>
> *"Reinvention and relevance in the 21st century instead draw on our ability to adjust our way of thinking, learning, doing, and being. Leaders must get comfortable with living in a state of continually becoming, a perpetual beta mode. Leaders that stay on top of society's changes do so by being receptive and able to learn."*[14]

Idea: How can you foster a learning environment inside your practice group? Could team meetings regularly include an interesting learning point (perhaps not always discipline related, it could be a personal development or behavioural skills issue) and encourage all team members from junior to leadership to take turns in sharing their recent learnings and even mistakes they have learnt from?

"Emotional intelligence" and an understanding of the impact on others

> *"When asked to define the ideal leader, many would emphasize traits such as intelligence, toughness, determination, and vision – the qualities traditionally associated with leadership... Although a certain degree of analytical and technical skill is a minimum requirement for success, studies indicate that emotional intelligence may be the key attribute that distinguishes outstanding performers from those who are merely adequate."*[15]

For generations, the legal profession has promoted its leaders based on expertise, intelligence, determination (or stickability). Emotional intelligence (or EQ) hasn't traditionally been something associated with attorneys and perhaps it was even seen as a flaw or a weakness in a challenging environment. Our leaders of the future are already displaying these so-called soft skills and awareness is growing of this vital trait for effective practice group leadership.

> *"The technical skills that helped secure your first promotion might not guarantee your next. If you aspire to be in a leadership role, there's an emotional element you need to consider. It's what helps you successfully coach teams, manage stress, deliver feedback, and collaborate with others… [It] accounts for nearly 90 percent of what sets high performers apart from peers with similar technical skills and knowledge."*[16]

Whilst emotional intelligence involves self-awareness and self-regulation to a large degree, it also encompasses the cultivating of great relationships, social skills, and empathy.

Trevor Sterling[17] explains, *"I have to look at everybody in my team as individuals. It is a nurturing and developing role, helping them to be the best they can be."*

Effective practice group leaders need to be aware of their own strengths and areas of growth plus those of their team members and promote those around them. They also know that they act as role models to the other team leaders of the group. It is important that the language and actions of the senior leaders match the narrative of the culture they are looking to create. Many leaders still lack the emotional intelligence to realize that the "Do as I say not as I do" approach is not particularly effective in building an engaged, open, and productive team.

In their book, Daniel Goleman, Richard Boyatzis, and Annie McKee say:

> *"The EI [emotional intelligence] competencies are not innate talents, but learned abilities, each of which has a unique contribution to making leaders more resonant, and therefore more effective."*[18]

Idea: Visit www.talentsmarteq.com/assessments/ (or a similar provider) and take your own assessment to see where you are currently in relation to your EQ levels. The report produced will identify areas of improvement for you to consider. If you engage a coach, they can help you to recognize where you can build on your skills and support you as you test out different leadership tools.

Truly embraces diversity and inclusivity within the team

> *"Diverse teams make better decisions up to 87 percent of the time… research shows that decision making effectiveness is 95 percent correlated with financial performance."*[19]

Diversity is not just the right thing to do. Diversity enhances creativity and thinking outside the box and increases retention and productivity. The legal profession exists to service a diverse range of clients, which should be reflected in those providing that service. Indeed, clients themselves are driving the agenda by asking organizations to disclose their diversity statistics. The group practice head takes a leading role in driving change.

Trevor Sterling is the first black senior partner at a top 100 UK law firm but realizes that this is just the start. He said to me:

> *"Yes, that [position as the first black senior partner] is fantastic. But the next thing is to see the second and the third ones coming through, that's the important thing. I've got to make sure that more people want to come into the law from diverse backgrounds. I engage with schools and universities. I'm working to ensure we have processes that allow people to come into our business, where they will not be subjected to unconscious bias in the selection and interview process. And then once they are here, they can move forward into leadership positions.*
>
> *"That's my approach in each and every issue that I'm trying to address. What are the challenges, what are the issues? How do I approach that or fix it? What do I do? The biggest challenge is getting others to think like that. Don't just talk about it, and just criticize it, but do something.*
>
> *"My individuality is my personality, and without personality, you lose a lot. In firms we talk in terms of branding, but don't talk in terms of personality. And for me that's really important. It comes from having a whole diverse range of people within your business."*[20]

Idea: Utilizing all the skills mentioned in this chapter will be necessary. In addition, consider the use of Employee Resource Groups (ERGs), with the full and clear support from you as practice group leader. Effective open and honest communication is key alongside the use of metrics to monitor improvement over time as new initiatives such as blind CVs are implemented.

In closing, it would be remiss not to mention that effective practice group leadership is not an easy task, and it is not always embraced to the full by those who take on the responsibility. By reading this book and adopting some of these ideas and concepts, you have taken a step further than many towards increasing your own skills in this vital area of your career. It is also important for law firms to provide effective training and support for their leadership teams and to consider the expectations placed on individuals in terms of fee earning and billables, versus spending their valuable time being an effective practice group leader.

References

1. https://lawcare-lifeinthelaw-v6-final.pdf
2. http://fs.blog/carol-dweck-mindset
3. *Ibid.*
4. Interview with Trevor Sterling, senior partner and head of the major trauma group at Moore Barlow on 16 February 2022.
5. Interview with Adrian Barker, global L&D manager and executive coach at Freshfields Bruckhaus Deringer on 16 February 2022.
6. www.tonyrobbins.com/mind-meaning/how-to-use-fear
7. See endnote 5.
8. https://hbr.org/2018/01/what-self-awareness-really-is-and-how-to-cultivate-it
9. https://www.apa.org/news/press/releases/2012/03/well-being
10. https://amycedmondson.com/
11. https://en.wikipedia.org/wiki/Maslow%27s_hierarchy_of_needs
12. Interview with Trish McLellan, director of research and engagement at LawCare on 4 March 2022, discussing the UK cases of Sovani James and Claire Matthews who were junior attorneys struck off the roll in 2018 and 2020 following investigations by the Solicitors Disciplinary Tribunal. www.saunders.co.uk/news/mental-health-problems-in-the-legal-profession-does-the-sra-sufficiently-recognise-the-pressures-on-lawyers. Claire Matthews' case is to be appealed following crowd funding by members of the profession. www.lawgazette.co.uk/news/struck-off-junior-solicitor-claire-matthews-to-have-case-re-heard-by-sdt/5107883.article
13. See endnote 5.
14. https://hbr.org/2015/10/the-best-leaders-are-constant-learners
15. https://hbr.org/2004/01/what-makes-a-leader
16. https://online.hbs.edu/blog/post/emotional-intelligence-in-leadership
17. See endnote 4.
18. Goleman, D., Boyatzis, R., and McKee, A., *Primal Leadership: Realizing the Power of Emotional Intelligence* (Boston: Harvard Business School Press, 2002), 38.
19. www.forbes.com/sites/eriklarson/2017/09/21/new-research-diversity-inclusion-better-decision-making-at-work
20. See endnote 4.

About Globe Law and Business

Globe Law and Business was established in 2005. From the very beginning, we set out to create law books which are sufficiently high level to be of real use to the experienced professional, yet still accessible and easy to navigate. Most of our authors are drawn from Magic Circle and other top commercial firms, both in the UK and internationally.

Our titles are carefully produced, with the utmost attention paid to editorial, design and production processes. We hope this results in high-quality publications that are easy to read, and a pleasure to own. Our titles are also available as ebooks, which are compatible with most desktop, laptop and tablet devices. In 2018 we expanded our portfolio to include journals and Special Reports, available both digitally and in hard copy format, and produced to the same high standards as our books.

In the spring of 2021, we were very pleased to announce the start of a new chapter for Globe Law and Business following the acquisition of law books under the imprint Ark Publishing. We are very much looking forward to working with our new Ark authors, many of whom are well known to us, to further developing the law firm management list, and to welcoming our new Ark customers.

We'd very much like to hear from you with your thoughts and ideas for improving what we offer. Please do feel free to email me at sian@globelawandbusiness.com with your views.

Sian O'Neill
Managing director
Globe Law and Business
www.globelawandbusiness.com

Lightning Source UK Ltd.
Milton Keynes UK
UKHW020028020622
403836UK00006B/1118